BUSINESS REPORTS:
SAMPLES FROM THE "REAL WORLD"

Selected and Introduced
by

WILLIAM E. RIVERS
Auburn University

PRENTICE-HALL, INC., ENGLEWOOD CLIFFS, NEW JERSEY 07632

Library of Congress Cataloging in Publication Data
Main entry under title:

Business reports.

    Includes index.
    1. Corporation reports--United States. 2. Business
report writing. I. Rivers, William E.
HG4028.B2B87   808'.066651021   80-39893
ISBN 0-13-107656-6

Editorial/production supervision by Esther S. Koehn
Cover design by Creative Impressions
Manufacturing buyer: Gordon Osbourne

Printed in the United States of America

10 9 8 7 6 5 4 3 2 1

Prentice-Hall International, Inc., *London*
Prentice-Hall of Australia Pty. Limited, *Sydney*
Prentice-Hall of Canada, Ltd., *Toronto*
Prentice-Hall of India Private Limited, *New Delhi*
Prentice-Hall of Japan, Inc., *Tokyo*
Prentice-Hall of Southeast Asia Pte. Ltd., *Singapore*
Whitehall Books Limited, *Wellington, New Zealand*

DEDICATED TO

LYNN W. DENTON

COLLEAGUE, ADVISER, FRIEND

CONTENTS

ACKNOWLEDGMENTS

I am indebted to many people for various kinds of assistance with this book. Among those who deserve particular thanks are Lynn Denton, who made suggestions on format and content, read parts of the manuscript, and offered general encouragement; Steve Gresham, who participated in the initial stages of soliciting reports from companies and who offered encouragement and suggestions as the project evolved; Barbara Fourier and Frances Henderson, who cheerfully accepted the task of retyping several of the reports reproduced in the collection; and my wife, Alicia, who encouraged and consoled me throughout the project, helped proofread and edit the manuscript, and put up with my schedule despite unusual demands on her time and energy including the birth of our second child.

The greatest measure of thanks, however, must go to the officers of the companies which provided sample reports for publication in this collection. Without their time-consuming efforts to locate and forward to me suitable reports this book would not have been possible. Although I cannot list all the individuals who helped provide reports, I can list the companies fortunate to have them as employees and generous enough to allow their reports to be published here.

AMF Corporation
American Bankers Life
Amoco Oil Company
Anchor Hocking Corporation
Armco Steel Corporation
Baldor Electric Company
Birmingham Trust National Bank
Boise Cascade Corporation
Bruno's Food Stores, Inc.
Carolina Casulty Insurance
    Company
Chart House, Inc.
The Chesapeake Corporation of
    Virginia
Cities Service Company
The Citizens and Southern
    National Bank of S. C.
ConAgra, Inc.
Crystal Oil Company
Deloitte Haskins & Sells
    (Houston, Texas)
Delta Air Lines, Inc.
Durr-Fillauer Medical, Inc.
Equifax, Inc.
Exxon Corporation
First Tennessee National Corp.
IBM Corporation
Lockheed Aircraft Corporation

Marathon Oil Company

Media General, Inc.

Morton-Norwich Products, Inc.

Murphy Oil Corporation

NCR Corporation

Pennwalt Corporation

Quaker Oats Company

Ruddick Corporation

Saunders Leasing

The Standard Oil Company (Ohio)

Storer Broadcasting Company

Tyson Foods, Inc.

United Virginia Bank

Whirlpool Corporation

INTRODUCTION

Some students planning careers in business seem to believe they will never be required to write reports once they
finish school. Others, even after completing business writing
courses, have only a very vague idea of what writing demands
they will face on the job. This book is an attempt to help
all of you in business report writing classes better understand just what report writing really is like in the business
world while at the same time helping you to develop your reading and writing skills.

The reports in this text came directly from successful
companies with well-known reputations; they are only a small
sample from among hundreds of reports sent in by companies
which responded to a request for materials that might be help-
ful to students in business report writing classes. Perhaps
knowing that many upper-level officials from these firms gave
their valuable time to assemble and submit reports for this
collection because they appreciate the importance of good
writing in their jobs will help you to sharpen your enthusiasm
as you work to develop your writing skills.

Usually, the best writers are readers who carefully evaluate the written materials they see. This book's method of
helping you become a better writer is to lead you to become an
"intentional" critic of everything you read, especially your
own writing. Being a critic in this sense does not mean necessarily "finding fault;" it means approaching what you read
with the intention of evaluating it as a piece of writing and
determining its strengths and weaknesses. To help you move
toward this goal, you will be given assignments which are
specifically designed to lead you to answer basic questions
about content, style, and organization in the reports in this
collection. Constantly and in a variety of ways you will be
asked to evaluate, to enumerate strengths and weaknesses in
the reports. Your learning to apply automatically this critical, questioning approach to what you read means that you will
also come to apply it to your own writing. Then, as your own

1

best critic, you will be able to continually improve and re-
fine your writing, not just for the short time you are in a
business writing course, but throughout your career. Writing,
like most sophisticated, useful skills, cannot be mastered
through a few courses in an academic setting; it must be stud-
ied and worked at all ones professional career. Hopefully, by
developing that critical approach to reading through "real
world" materials, you will find it easier to transfer that at-
titude from an academic to a professional ("real world") setting and thus ensure your continued development as an effective
writer.

The collection of reports here is a good sample of those
you will encounter later; however, it should not be considered
representative of all the types of reports written in the business world, for several reasons. First, in order to be econo-
mically reasonable as a supplimentary text, the book had to be
carefully limited in length. In selecting the reports included
here I was guided by these considerations: to produce an economical text containing as many business reports as possible
which would (1) cover a broad range of topics and purposes,
(2) come from companies varying in size and business, and (3)
be both interesting and intelligible to students. To meet the
criteria for quanity, variety, and economy, I have preferred
shorter reports to longer ones. Although this policy did require me to omit some interesting longer reports, the prefer-
ence for shorter reports is one that you will encounter in the
business world. Longer reports--especially the long, formal
reports that occupy such a prominent position in business writing texts--are required much less frequently than the shorter,
informal memo reports; they are the reports that get the
world's work done. Furthermore, if you are asked to write one
of these longer, more formal reports, that request will probably not come early in your career. They are usually assigned
to more experienced employees who have demonstrated their ana-
lytical and writing skills through shorter reports.

Second, while the 38 companies whose reports were used to
form this collection are a good cross-section of the business
community, the particular types of reports they sent may not
be the ones most common in their own or the thousands of other
companies across the U.S. You should realize that the need
for confidentiality often played a part in determining which
reports were sent. Company officials could send only reports
that would not compromise or divulge sensitive positions, operations, or procedures of their companies. In some cases,
company officials dealt with this need by sending reports that
were typical but not current; others changed or omitted names
and/or figures. Because of their time-consuming efforts to
protect their companies' interests while providing you with

2

typical reports, you can be sure that the sample is a good one, but you should realize that many other interesting kinds of reports await your reading and writing in the "real world."

To provide you with reports that are as authentic as possible, I have made every effort to present them as they originally appeared. They have been edited in only a very few places, with very minor changes. In a few cases reports required retyping to produce dark, clear copies for reproduction or to make changes necessary to ensure confidentiality; even then, their original formats and appearance were adhered to as closely as possible.

I am firmly convinced that having these reports in their original forms can be an invaluable aid in your study of business report writing. However, you must be aware of one pitfall to guard against in this method of presentation. You are accustomed to business writing texts which contain "model" reports written or carefully rewritten by the textbook authors to give you examples to use as patterns in your own writing. Therefore, you may be expecting the reports in this book to be the best possible specimens of good writing and principles of presentation. That expectation, however, cannot be met in a collection designed to give you contact with genuine reports from the business world. Although business executives emphatically emphasize to their employees the importance of clear, concise, error-free reports, they realize that under the stringent pressures of "real world" deadlines there will inevitably be some lapses of good writing practice. The reports in this book, simply because they are "real," do contain some mistakes in grammar and punctuation and, in some people's judgment, mistakes in style and organization. Consequently, you must be aware more than ever of correct usage and good writing practices; otherwise, you may find yourself using errors as guides.

Rather than seeing these reports as "models," you should look on them as samples that illustrate many strenghts and some weaknesses in report writing. Approached in this way, they can be quite effective tools in helping you improve your writing skills and gain confidence in your ability to use those skills successfully.

3

A NOTE ON THE SECTION AND REPORT INTRODUCTIONS

Because of the need to devote as much space as possible to reports and my desire to allow your instructor as much flexibility as possible in using these reports, the introductory materials for sections and reports are brief. The section introductions are intended to orient you to the common characteristics and functions of the reports in each section and should not be considered attempts to define these report types in a definitive way.

The introductions to individual reports focus on the company for which the report was written and then on the report itself. The information on the contributing companies (the nature of its business, the location of its headquarters, and, when available, the number of its employees) was taken from Standard & Poor's Register of Corporations, Directors, and Executives (Vol. I, Standard & Poor's Corporation: New York, 1980). In some cases additional information provided by individual companies has been included. The introductory comments on each report briefly summarize the report and direct your attention to particular characteristics of each report as a way of drawing you into it; you should not, however, restrict your attention as you read solely to these characteristics. Your instructor will provide additional information on report types and guidance on special things to look for in the reports.

I. STATUS REPORTS

Status reports can be divided into two basic types: regular periodic reports (or activity reports) and special status reports.

Regular periodic reports, probably the type of report most frequently written in the business world, are summaries of the routine activities of individuals or departments within a business. Depending on the nature of the business conducted by the company and the segment of that business handled by the reporting individual or department, periodic status reports may be submitted weekly, biweekly, or monthly and, in some cases, quarterly or annually. These reports usually follow a standarized format so that upper level managers can quickly review the activities of many people and departments. The standardized formats and the detailed, often cryptically presented information can make regular periodic reports seem monotonous to an uninitiated reader. But to the conscientious manager, regular periodic reports hold the monotonous fascination of a heartbeat for they are valuable indicators of the whole organization's health.

Because special status reports deal with unusual circumstances, they vary greatly in format and content and often must provide fuller explanations than those found in regular periodic reports. They are, therefore, ususally more interesting than regular reports. Despite this basic difference, both special status reports and regular periodic reports serve the same function of keeping managers--even corporate directors-- informed about the company's operation and health.

In this section you will find examples of both regular periodic reports and special status reports.

I. STATUS REPORTS

1. Status-Systems & Programming

2. Activity Report for the period
   ending March 4, 1977

   (Crystal Oil Company)

THE COMPANY: With its headquarters in Shreveport,
                Louisiana, Crystal Oil Company employs
                approximately 430 people in the produc-
                tion of oil and gas.

THE REPORTS: These two regular periodic reports bring
    (2)   the managers of Crystal Oil Company up
                to date on the progress in two important
                departments. The first is a report from
                the data processing center on its pro-
                gress in converting company operations
                to a new computer system. The second is
                a report on the credit department's ac-
                tivities with an emphasis on its efforts
                to collect past due accounts. (Some
                names have been deleted from Report #2.)

CRYSTAL OIL COMPANY

MEMO

TO _Jerry Davidson_   FROM _Charles Spearman_

RE _Status-Systems & Programming_   DATE _March 7, 1977_

The conversion project is proceeding on schedule. We have a tentative distribution plan for the CRT terminals, however, we are not going to be able to make a final decision on placement until we actually start converting. Looking at our terminal requirements it is very possible we will need additional CRT's for Personnel and the Production Departments as we develop systems for them.

We are still awaiting final documentation on the Accounts Receivable System before making presentations to the Accounting Departments on receivables. Most of the file conversion specifications for accounting history data have been defined and conversion programs are being written. Requested modifications on Accounts Payable have been completed and documentation is complete.

A recap of programming effort follows:

Bill Martin is working with Personnel on design of a Personnel data base. He has written an interim data capture program that will provide Personnel with a mini data base while the system is being designed.

Ric Jones made a presentation of the Royalty & Revenue System to a group from Production last week. Ric is in the process of making modifications requested by E & P Accounting and remains about 95% complete. He has been delayed on design of the Joint Interest System because of the modifications required to Royalty & Revenue. Work should begin on Joint Interest this week.

Tom Bannister continues to program the month end accounting reports for Refinery Accounting. He is 50% complete with this project.

Bill Dollar is working on the initial conversion steps for converting accounting history. The final steps cannot be completed until we have our equipment installed.

Charles Spearman
Charles Spearman

CS/tw

CRYSTAL OIL COMPANY

MEMO

TO Bryce Crider

FROM Charles J. McComb, Jr.

RE Activity Report for the period
ending March 4, 1977

DATE March 4, 1977

I. <u>Stone Companies</u>

    (A) _____ - Efforts to collect the Holland Flying Service note have not been successful. Our attorney advises that all amicable avenues have been exhausted and suit is being filed. You may remember, Barfield gave us this note as an on-account payment on his past-due account last year.

        After a Motion to Compel was filed against Barfield, we finally received the Answer and Counterclaims. A copy is before Sharon Hawke now for advice and handling.

    (B) <u>Dari-Delite</u> - At their request, we have made an offer to sell the property to Dari-International. Our offer involves a 25% cash down-payment and financing the balance. We are waiting for their reaction to our offer.

II. _____

    (A) _____ - Suit for non-payment was filed in federal court, Little Rock, Arkansas on February 22, 1977 for $158,815.00. On February 28 we forwarded new affidavits to our attorney to file an amendment to reflect the adjusted balance of $152,101.85. We are optimistic that we will collect this account, but it may take some time, principally due to the backlog in the courts. A trial date could be 6-12 months away. Meanwhile, we are continuing to apply as much pressure as we legally can. Interrogatories and Request for Admissions are being drafted. We are also looking into the feasibility of filing an injunction to prevent the sale of certain assets.

    (B) _____ - Mr. Shore had requested credit in order to purchase 20-25 loads of diesel a month. This base period customer has not met our standards, and we therefore declined to comply with his request. Primarily our decision is based on his disregard for established credit terms, specifically of taking illegal discounts.

III. <u>Rico</u>

    (A) <u>U.S. National Metals, Inc.</u> - No change.

    (B) <u>Aztec Industries</u> - No change.

Bryce Crider
Page 2
March 4, 1977

IV. CPC

    (A) Nichols Oil Co. - No change.

V. Crystal Oil

    (A) _____ - Our attorney attended the creditors'
          meeting on February 14, 1977. Much of the information presented
          by them was deemed to be understated or unreliable. Their intent
          is to form a Creditors' Committee to pay off the many creditors.
          At this point in time, we view their plan as a classic case of chaos.

    (B) Joint Interest Accounts - As we reported last time, our past due
          list of 39 accounts totaling $23,833.43 has been reduced by 9 accounts
          for $6,726.88. We are continuing to work with Bill McBride to
          resolve the rest of them.

In summary, we remain hopeful.

Charles J. McComb, Jr.

CJM/csc

I. STATUS REPORTS

3.   December Automobile Finance Report

         (Anonymous)

THE COMPANY: This report was provided by a major region-
                  al bank located in a Southeastern state.

THE REPORT: The following document is a standard,
                  monthly status report designed to give
                  bank officers a quick but detailed pic-
                  ture of the bank's success in a particular
                  segment of its financial market--in this
                  case automobiles loans. In periodic re-
                  ports this ratio of verbal analysis and
                  summary to graphs and tables (1 page to
                  5 pages) is fairly common. (The abbre-
                  viation "AB" in the report stands for
                  "A Bank.")

actiongram

marketing information of timely importance

*vol:*IV *no:*3 *date:*2-18-77 *distribution:* EXECUTIVE MANAGEMENT,
CITY EXECUTIVE, MARKETING
subject: DECEMBER AUTOMOBILE OFFICERS, SYSTEM ILD
FINANCE REPORT OFFICERS, FUNCTIONAL HEADS

DECEMBER
SALES

In December AB had 545 new car loans for 2.6 million with
the average loans being $4,852. This compares to one year
ago in December of 1975 when 515 new car loans were made with
the average loan being $4,777.

Below is a chart of year to date figures for AB new car
loans made either at a AB branch or with a dealer.

	DIRECT	%	DEALER	%	TOTAL
1976	3322	39.3	5122	60.7	8444
1975	2774	42.8	3706	57.2	6480
1974	1521	38.5	2428	61.5	3949

The total number of loans increased by 113.8% in 1976 over
1974. The percentage of Direct Loans as compared to the
total has increased slightly from 38.5% in 1974 to 39.3%
in 1976.

PAYMENT
STRETCHER
LOANS

Payment Stretcher Loans accounted for 24.2% of the total
number of new car loans made in December. Direct Stretcher
Loans represented 49.2% of the total. For the entire year
of 1976, 22.2% of all new car loans made where Payment
Stretcher Loans. This compares to 14.7% in 1975 and 11.3%
in 1974.

MARKET SHARE

The AB adjusted Market Share was 9.9% for December or
down .1% from November. The actual for the current month
was 8.4%

USED CAR
LOANS

There were 642 Used Car Loans made in December for $1.4
million. Direct Used Car Loans represented 78.0% of the
total number.

New Auto Loans as a Percent of
New Auto Registrations in Counties
Served by C&S:

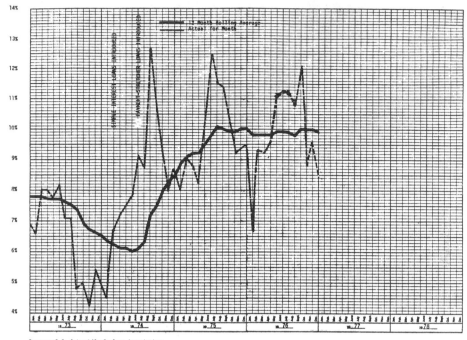

Sources: S.C. Automobile Dealers Association;
ILD New and Used Auto Report

MARKET SHARE

COUNTY	REGISTRATIONS	C&S CITY	DECEMBER 1976 NUMBER OF C&S NEW CAR LOANS	DECEMBER 1976 NET NEW CAR REGISTRATIONS	DECEMBER 1976 MARKET SHARE
Anderson	373	Anderson	17	373	4.6
Berkeley	231	Camden	16	85	18.8
Charleston	1,018	Charleston	118	1,448	8.1
Cherokee	90	Columbia	84	1,517	5.5
Darlington	127	Conway/ MB	69	397	17.4
Dorchester	199	Flor/Darl	33	461	7.2
Florence	334	Gaffney	26	90	28.9
Greenville	955	Greenville	54	955	5.7
Horry	397	Orangeburg	23	198	11.6
Kershaw	85	Rock Hill	38	313	12.1
Lexington	485	Spartanburg	46	429	10.7
Orangeburg	198	Sumter	21	227	9.3
Richland	1,032				
Sumter	227				
Spartanburg	429	TOTAL	545	6,493	8.4
York	313				
TOTAL	6,493				

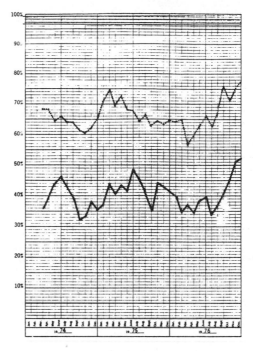

──────── PERCENTAGE OF DIRECT LOANS ON NEW CARS MADE EACH MONTH

········ PERCENTAGE OF DIRECT LOANS ON USED CARS MADE EACH MONTH

MONTHLY REPORT ON
NEW & USED
AUTOMOBILE LOANS
DECEMBER

SYSTEM	NEW						USED					
	DIRECT	Change	INDIRECT	Change	TOTAL	Change	DIRECT	Change	INDIRECT	Change	TOTAL	Change
1974	109		198		307		269		135		404	
1975	201	92 84.4	284	86 43.4	485	178 58.0	340	71 26.4	185	50 37.0	525	121 30.0
1976	284	83 41.3	261	(23) (8.1)	545	60 12.4	501	161 47.4	141	(44) (23.8)	642	117 22.3

Source: ILD New and Used Auto Report

Prepared by Marketing Research

13

INSTALLMENT LOANS FOR AUTOMOBILES
DECEMBER, 1976

| City | DIRECT LOANS | | | | | | DEALER LOANS | | | | | | ALL | |
| | 36 MONTHS OR LESS | | OVER 36 MONTHS | | TOTAL DIRECT | | 36 MONTHS OR LESS | | OVER 36 MONTHS | | TOTAL DEALER | | TOTAL NEW CAR LOANS | |
	Number	Dollars	Number	Dollars	Number	Dollars	Number	Dollars	Number	Dollars	Number	Dollars	Number	Dollars
Anderson	6	30,116	4	20,421	10	50,537	3	15,169	4	25,753	7	40,922	17	91,459
Camden	5	22,100	2	12,004	7	34,104	4	19,063	5	29,470	9	48,533	16	82,637
Charleston	50	191,128	15	81,710	65	272,838	39	191,882	14	80,005	53	271,887	118	544,725
Columbia	43	206,094	8	39,272	51	245,366	27	133,843	6	38,048	33	171,891	84	417,257
Florence	12	54,361	9	42,363	21	96,724	9	47,208	3	17,723	12	64,931	33	161,655
Gaffney	16	63,247	3	17,127	19	80,374	2	13,969	5	31,636	7	45,605	26	125,979
Greenville	20	80,267	4	20,231	24	100,498	22	115,337	8	47,196	30	162,533	54	263,031
M/Beach	20	89,659	6	34,618	26	124,277	33	165,584	10	64,840	43	230,424	69	354,701
Orangeburg	7	28,619	2	8,803	9	37,422	8	42,150	6	41,060	14	83,210	23	120,632
Rock Hill	19	83,575	2	12,329	21	95,904	15	73,727	2	13,652	17	87,379	38	183,283
Spartanburg	15	59,569	2	8,802	17	68,371	26	124,493	3	19,385	29	143,878	46	212,249
Sumter	6	24,744	8	37,776	14	62,520	6	20,127	1	4,081	7	24,208	21	86,728
System	219	933,479	65	335,456	284	1,268,935	194	962,552	67	412,849	261	1,375,401	545	2,644,336
AVERAGE LOAN		4,262		5,161		4,468		4,962		6,162		5,270		4,852

NUMBER OF INSTALLMENT LOANS
FOR NEW AUTOMOBILES
DECEMBER, 1976

City	DIRECT LOANS									DEALER LOANS									ALL					
	36 MONTHS OR LESS			OVER 36 MONTHS			TOTAL DIRECT			36 MONTHS OR LESS			OVER 36 MONTHS			TOTAL DEALER			TOTAL NEW CAR LOANS			% OVER 36 MONTHS		
	This Month	Last Month	To Date	This Month	Last Month	To Date	This Month	Last Month	To Date	This Month	Last Month	To Date	This Month	Last Month	To Date	This Month	Last Month	To Date	This Month	Last Month	To Date	This Month	Last Month	To Date
Anderson	6	7	120	4	2	52	10	9	172	3	5	73	4	4	47	7	9	120	17	18	292	47.1	33.3	33.9
Camden	5	5	57	2	4	24	7	9	81	4	17	161	5	3	47	9	20	208	16	29	289	43.8	24.1	24.6
Charleston	50	43	444	15	11	130	65	54	574	39	36	675	14	4	184	53	40	859	118	94	1,433	24.5	16.0	21.9
Columbia	43	40	532	8	8	131	51	48	663	27	31	641	6	6	129	33	37	770	84	85	1,433	16.7	16.5	19.1
Florence	12	21	196	9	4	74	21	25	270	9	6	235	3	2	72	12	8	307	33	33	577	36.4	18.2	25.3
Gaffney	16	12	179	3	4	48	19	16	227	2	9	154	5	3	63	7	12	217	26	28	444	30.8	25.0	25.1
Greenville	20	23	250	4	4	62	24	27	312	22	35	648	8	0	21	30	35	669	54	62	981	22.2	6.5	8.5
M/Beach	20	18	197	6	11	101	26	29	298	33	26	425	10	4	199	43	30	624	69	59	922	23.2	25.4	32.5
Orangeburg	7	7	75	2	4	36	9	11	111	8	6	182	6	11	98	14	17	280	23	28	391	34.8	53.6	34.3
Rock Hill	19	10	172	2	1	18	21	11	190	15	8	135	2	5	51	17	13	186	38	24	376	10.5	25.0	18.4
Spartanburg	15	17	227	2	4	62	17	21	289	26	20	607	3	8	160	29	28	767	46	49	1,056	10.9	24.5	21.0
Sumter	6	4	84	8	3	51	14	7	135	6	8	102	1	0	13	7	8	115	21	15	250	42.9	20.0	25.6
System	219	207	2,533	65	60	789	284	267	3,322	194	207	4,038	67	50	1,084	261	257	5,122	545	524	8,444	24.2	21.0	22.2

15

I. STATUS REPORTS

4. Energy Curtailment/Transportation
   Shortage Impact Report

   (Whirlpool Corporation)

THE COMPANY: With headquarters in Benton Harbor, Mich-
                 igan, Whirlpool is a manufacturer and mar-
                 keter of a full line of major home appli-
                 ances. The company is also the primary
                 supplier of major home appliances to
                 Sears, Roebuck and Company. Whirlpool
                 employs 23,573 people.

THE REPORT: A summary of the impact of energy short-
                 ages and heavy snow storms on Whirlpool's
                 operations, this report illustrates the
                 need for concise summaries of data beyond
                 standard periodic reports. Notice that
                 the report begins with an overview of
                 Whirlpool operations and then summarizes
                 the situation in each division.

 **Whirlpool** CORPORATION

Administrative Center

BENTON HARBOR, MICHIGAN 49022

February 16, 1978

TO: Officers and General Managers

FROM: Andy Takacs

SUBJECT: Energy Curtailment/Transprotation Shortage Impact
           Report

Attached is an update on the report on the impact of the
electricity shortage on the company sent to you on February 2,
1978. We've also condensed it considerably this time around.

If you have any questions on any part of it, please feel free
to call me, Steve Sizer or Carol Zerler.

AJT/d

Attachment

cc: S. Upton
       DIR's
       Communicators

17

SUMMARY - 2/16/78

Electricity

The coal strike and resulting electricity shortages threaten
problems for all Whirlpool operations, but all able to maintain
normal production schedules to present.

Marion only division with mandatory curtailment so far, but
with help of diesel air compressors, plus elimination of all
non-essential electrical use, able to maintain 5 day, 8 hour
shift production. Curtailment now 25% ... could go to 50%
February 21 ... but addition of diesel generators expected to
permit continuation of near normal operations. Curtailment to
maintenance levels now expected around 3/1 will force cessation
of all production except parts for other divisions.

All divisions report no problems with other fuels...but diesel
fuel shortages may develop as more and more manufacturers turn
to auxiliary generators in short supply due to sudden increased
demand.

Already high energy costs will rise even more at plants using
generators, due to high fuel costs and lease charges ... but
better than shutting down.

All divisions conserving electricity to fullest extent possible
short of disrupting production. Planned production increases
postponed or delayed at most divisions.

Transportation

Bigger problem now is lack of transportation due to snow
storms. Trucks and box cars in short supply...available equipment strained beyond capacity...maintenance problems occurring.

All divisions report some back-ups of finished goods. Most
report storage areas full, PD warehouses full. Current estimates 4 to 5 weeks to return to normal, assuming no more
storms.

Whirlpool distributor and branch warehouses low on merchandise
... 2/17 price increase on Whirlpool brand announced last month
delayed to 3/13.

Divisions still receiving vendor parts in time to maintain
production, but touch and go, day-to-day proposition. Schedule
changes, air freight, own trucks being used to keep things
moving.

CLYDE DIVISION

Electricity

No curtailment at present. Toledo Edison has 49 day coal
supply and is receiving more. Production levels normal, but
planned increase for 2/20 postponed, affecting status of 230
people just hired. Voluntary conservation plan in effect.

Product Shipments

Transportation equipment shortages hampering finished goods
shipments. Storage areas full to overflowing.

Vendor Parts

Supplies still coming in, but erratic. Demands day-to-day
watching, schedule changes and the like. Problem may grow
worse as vendors experience curtailments.

FINDLAY DIVISION

Electricity

No curtailment at present. Ohio Power has 52 day coal supply
and is receiving more. Forty day level will bring voluntary
curtailment, 30 day level will bring mandatory 10%
curtailment. Outlook good for now. No production problems ...
Saturday 2/11 worked, 2/18 planned. Voluntary conservation
plan in effect.

Product Shipments

Severe shortages of trucks and rail cars hampering shipments of
finished goods. PD warehouse and storage areas full.

Vendor Parts

Still having problems getting vendor parts as needed. Schedule
changes, air freight, own trucks being used to accommodate.

MARION DIVISION

Electricity

Hardest hit so far, but responding well. 25% curtailment in
effect, 50% curtailment due 2/21, maintenance levels expected
about 3/1.

Ohio Edison down to 36 day coal supply, but will reserve extra power from grid next week, which will support 25% curtailment levels. No word on extra power beyond that.

With aid of four diesel air compressors and 250 KW generators for warehouse, Marion can support near-normal production levels while on 50% curtailment.

Marion has leased two 650 KW diesel generators to be on line 3/1. This will support production of parts for other divisions when electricity is curtailed to maintenance levels.

Marion currently maintaining 5 day, 8 hour shift schedules. Expect to sustain this level until electricity curtailed to maintenance levels.

Other Fuels

No problems...except possible shortage of diesel fuel as more and more manufacturers opt to generate their own power.

Product Shipments

Severe shortages of trucks and freight cars hampering shipments. PD warehouse and plant storage areas full of finished goods awaiting shipment.

Vendor Parts

Vendor part deliveries still delayed. A day-to-day situation, but able to accommodate so far.

Other Problems

Shortage of storage bins for parts. Self-generated power much more expensive than utility power.

ST. JOSEPH DIVISION

Electricity

Voluntary 25% curtailment imposed by I & M today ... may be mandatory next week. I & M has less than 50 day coal supply, but is receiving coal. Outlook in doubt.

Product Shipments

Some difficulty with transportation equipment shortages, but not backed up yet. Parts to other divisions still moving.

Page 3

Vendor Parts

Only moderate delays, some schedule changes. Alternates being
sought for vendors affected by electricity curtailments.

Other Problems

Possibility of shortage of parts from Marion due to power
problems there. Shortage of bins used to transport parts to
other divisions, and to store parts.

DANVILLE DIVISION

Electricity

Scheduled production continues at Danville. Use of electricity
has been voluntarily cut back 10% and they continue to look for
other ways to conserve. No word from the supplier on need to
reduce further. If it comes, production expected to be
affected.

Product Shipment

Trucks continue to be available for handling product
shipments.

Vendor Parts

There is a two day supply of parts-in-plant, down from the
normal 5-day reserve.

EVANSVILLE DIVISION

Electricity

Under 25% voluntary curtailment. All non-essential usage
eliminated. No mandatory curtailment until SIGEGO falls below
40 day coal supply. Indiana has called up National Guard to
keep non-union coal moving, which means SIGECO should continue
to receive coal. Evansville maintaining normal schedule, but
plans to add about 900 people now being re-examined. Current
outlook for electricity still good.

Product Shipments

Shipments hampered by equipment shortages, but storage
facilities not yet full.

Page 4

Vendor Parts

Still receiving as needed, with some schedule adjustments
required. Looking for alternate vendors as electricity
curtailments in Ohio begin to cause concern.

FORT SMITH DIVISION

Electricity

Electricity availability stable. No problems anticipated
unless required to share coal supplies. They are going ahead
with a planned schedule increase on 2/20 that will result in
the recall of 190 previously laid off employees.

Product Shipments

Some shortage of rail cars due to latest winter storm that hit
the northeast. No serious problem at this time.

Vendor Parts

Biggest concern at Ft. Smith is availability of parts from
Indiana and Ohio vendors...including Whirlpool Divisions. They
have been able to maintain production so far, but future
uncertain.

ST. PAUL DIVISION

Electricity

Reports no shortages or impending curtailments. All activities
functioning at normal levels.

Product Shipments

Minor difficulties experienced ... not serious.

Vendor Parts

Experiencing erratic deliveries, but not enough to force
schedule adjustments yet. Also experiencing some difficulty
receiving materials.

LAPORTE DIVISION

Electricity

LaPorte voluntarily has reduced electrical energy use as much as possible without cutting back operations. NIPSCO, their supplier, has a 65 day coal supply but may have to "share" energy as situations in other areas of the State worsen.

Product Shipments

Trucks and rail cars are getting to the plant to pick up out-going orders though time in transit to customers has been extended.

Vendor Parts

Vendor parts supplies are adequate despite some backorders on purchased parts.

ADMINISTRATIVE CENTER

Electricity

As of 2/15, on voluntary 25% curtailment, at I & M request, with specific conservation steps issued and in effect.

I.   STATUS REPORTS

    5.   Refining, Marketing and Transportation

          (Cities Service Company)

THE COMPANY: Cities Service Company produces and markets
                  crude and refined oils, chemicals, plas-
                  tics, natural gas, and copper. Company
                  headquarters are in Tulsa, Oklahoma. The
                  company employs 18,100 people.

THE REPORT: This report is a detailed overview of
                  Cities Service's refining, marketing, and
                  transportation operations with an emphasis
                  on how Cities Service Company's operations
                  fit into those of the whole industry.
                  Since the report was written with a very
                  special internal and external audience
                  (the Board of Directors and professional
                  business analysts) in mind, it is neces-
                  sarily more formal and polished than most
                  internal business reports.

CITIES SERVICE COMPANY
COMMENTS FOR ANALYSTS

REFINING, MARKETING AND TRANSPORTATION

APRIL, 1977

Reports of various phases of Cities Service Company's operations are made periodically to the Board of Directors. These presentations contain pertinent information that we believe would be of interest to professional analysts.

This report discusses the Company's Refining, Marketing and Transportation activities. Similar reports on other operations will be furnished to you subsequent to their presentation to the Board.

Sterling McKittrick, Jr.
Vice President, Investor Affairs

REFINING, MARKETING AND TRANSPORTATION

Industry Review - Downstream Activities

     In the past, converting crude oil production into dollars has
been the name of the game with downstream activities being marginally
profitable. Today, we compete in a world where there are too many
refineries, too many retail outlets, too many tankers, too little crude
oil supply with too much of it in one spot, too much oil demand with
too little incentive to develop alternatives, and too much government
help in running our business. It is very difficult to predict the rules
governing the game we are trying to play. Within that environment,
we plan to chart a course that will let us succeed in our mission.

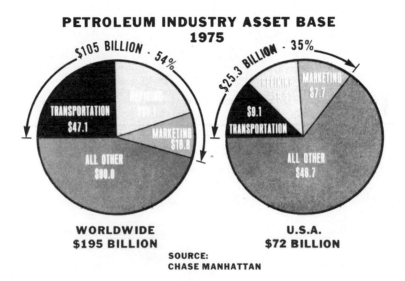

PETROLEUM INDUSTRY ASSET BASE
1975

$105 BILLION - 54%

$25.3 BILLION - 35%

TRANSPORTATION $47.1

REFINING $90.7

MARKETING $18.8

ALL OTHER $90.0

REFINING $8.5

MARKETING $7.7

$9.1 TRANSPORTATION

ALL OTHER $46.7

WORLDWIDE
$195 BILLION

U.S.A.
$72 BILLION

SOURCE:
CHASE MANHATTAN

     Worldwide, the asset base of the petroleum industry is $195
billion--about $72 billion here in the U.S. Investments downstream
constitute half of the assets worldwide but only 35 percent in the U.S.
This reflects our dependence on foreign refineries and tankers as well
as higher domestic E&P costs.

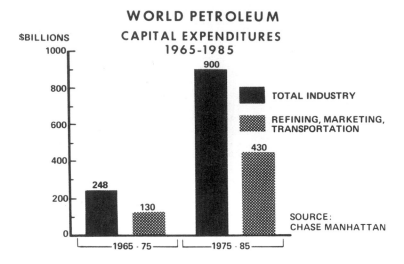

WORLD PETROLEUM
CAPITAL EXPENDITURES
1965-1985

$BILLIONS

TOTAL INDUSTRY

REFINING, MARKETING, TRANSPORTATION

SOURCE: CHASE MANHATTAN

1965 - 75   1975 - 85

The capital requirements for the industry are huge. Investments will quadruple during the 1975-85 decade compared with the previous ten years. Downstream activities will require about half the worldwide estimate and about 37 percent of the U.S. total.

U. S. PETROLEUM INDUSTRY
CAPITAL EXPENDITURES
1965-1985

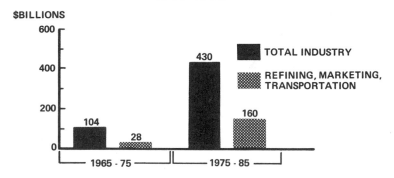

$BILLIONS

TOTAL INDUSTRY

REFINING, MARKETING, TRANSPORTATION

1965 - 75   1975 - 85

SOURCE: CHASE MANHATTAN

We expect oil demand to average 50 million barrels a day this year finally exceeding 1973--the year of the embargo. No doubt the recent OPEC price moves will again dampen demand to some extent. The 1980 number we are using is 55 million barrels a day and is probably on the low side of most forecasts. That is an increase of just under 2 million barrels daily each year from this point.

Eighty-three percent of the world oil reserves are held by the OPEC nations or the communists. Oil analysts tell us that OPEC's existing producing capacity is 38 million barrels of oil a day. In November 1976 it reached 33 million. We think a 34 million barrel per day average will be required to fill the 1977 demand.

Europe and the U.S. are clearly the world refining leaders. The refining capacity of the free world is about 60 million barrels a day which is 5 - 6 million more than needed. European and Caribbean plants have been operating at only 60 - 70 percent of capacity. The U.S. is averaging more than 90 percent.

Refining, Marketing and Transportation is responsible for Cities Service Company's oil operations from the wellhead to the consumer--the downstream activities of the Company. Details of these operations are presented in the remainder of this booklet.

Cities Service Petroleum Product Status

Now for some of our measurements. Within the 20 largest oil companies, we rank 16th in gasoline sales, 17th in distillate sales, and 18th in refining capacity. We are recognized as a "major" oil company by many, but there are at least three so-called "independents" that are bigger than we are in terms of refining capacity and sales. Being grouped with the majors is certainly not an advantage to us--nor does the designation properly reflect that marketing image we are trying to achieve.

The contribution to profit from downstream oil activities has been substantially influenced by price controls and government regulations. We have been subjected to some kind of price controls and product allocations since 1972. Gasoline, turbine fuel, and NGL products are still controlled. Our track record over the last five years has not been good. Our earnings results have been obviously inadequate to support the amount of investment and risk associated with the business. We do believe that we have done as well as most of our competitors over this period.

Contribution to Profit
Refining, Marketing and Transportation
(before interest expense, income taxes
and minority interest)

	$ Millions	Percent of Cities Service Company
1976	52.1	11
1975	(6.2)	(2)
1974	25.8	7
1973	25.1	11
1972	2.3	2

Our 1976 results were encouraging. The $52.1 million contribution from refining, marketing and transportation exceeded the achievements of the preceding four years combined. The turnaround in the earnings picture was the result of a more streamlined organization, a record performance by the refinery, and better price spreads at the wholesale level on essentially every product. Sales volume in 1976 was about 5 percent higher than 1975. However, a big difference in the two years was our ability to produce more of what we sold, thereby minimizing the purchase of finished products from others.

A number of items continue to concern us. These include labor negotiations, price controls, intense competition at retail, our ability to control operating costs, and the wide disparity in the cost of domestic and foreign crude. New concepts of planning, accounting and budget control are still being implemented to support our responsibility to the overall profitability of the Company. Cost control is vital and every effort is being made in that direction. Our employees have sacrificed much to achieve our progress to date and we feel their efforts will give us excellent support in competing on a profitable basis in the future.

Lubricants and Specialty Products

The Lubricants and Specialty Products unit was created under the reorganization last spring and, for the first time, control of the manufacture and sales of lubricants and specialty products has been centralized. Our operation has substantial value to the Company as profit possibilities are increased by the reformulation, packaging and distribution activities we conduct before products reach the ultimate marketplace.

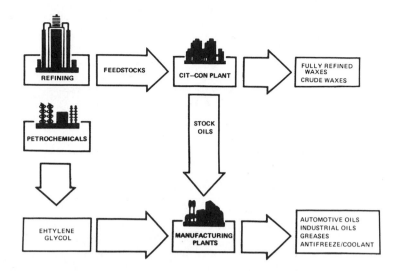

We purchase feedstocks from the Lake Charles refinery which are processed through Cit-Con Oil Corporation (65 percent Cities Service) to make high quality lubricating base stock oils and waxes. These products are sold either direct from Cit-Con to other refiners or moved to a series of owned and contracted manufacturing plants. At these plants, the stock oils are compounded and blended into CITGO automotive and industrial oils and greases. Ethylene glycol is manufactured into CITGO antifreeze and coolant.

This production, combined with tires, batteries and accessories purchased from outside major manufacturers, gives us an extensive

product line. We supply customers six separate grades of lubricating base stock oils; fully refined and crude waxes; over 200 separate automotive and industrial lubricants; CITGO antifreeze and coolant and major TBA lines.

Lubricants and Specialty Products was assigned responsibility for the Cit-Con plant at Lake Charles, the Cicero, Illinois compounding and blending plant, and product development facilities at Cranbury, New Jersey. The underlying asset total is some $51 million.

The Cit-Con plant has a finished stock oil capacity of 10,000 barrels per day. It can also produce 1,800 barrels per day of waxes.

The plant is presently operating at a higher rate of capacity than in the recent years due to increased demand.

Our Cicero plant has capacity to compound, blend and package approximately 50 million gallons of oils and greases per year. This plant currently is operating at a competitive level and we expect this to continue. From this plant, we were innovative some years ago in introducing bulk transport deliveries of grease.

Our products development laboratory at Cranbury has effected substantial savings in product formulation and made contributions to the Company's leading position in waxes, water glycol fire resistant fluids and two-cycle engine oils.

Our objectives and strategies have been established to develop and expand sales of manufactured products to utilize plants at higher rates and maximize our profit potential. We completed 1976 at a ratio of 56 percent stock oils and 44 percent finished oils and plan by 1980 to reverse our past record and produce two-thirds finished oils and one-third stock oils.

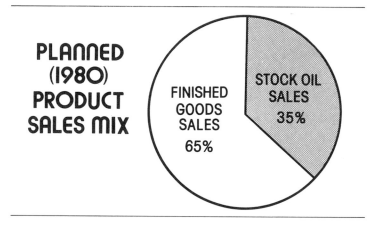

PLANNED (1980) PRODUCT SALES MIX

FINISHED GOODS SALES 65%

STOCK OIL SALES 35%

The lubricants and specialty products market in which we compete -- tires, batteries, accessories, lubricants, waxes and antifreeze is sizable and growing. Through our existing manufacturing and distribution facilities, we have the capability to reach approximately 60 percent of the total national market of $31.6 billion. With our facilities and purchasing arrangements, we are in a position to increase our share of this market with a minimum of new capital. Estimated annual growth rates range from 1 percent to 1-1/2 percent for lubes and up to 6 percent for accessories.

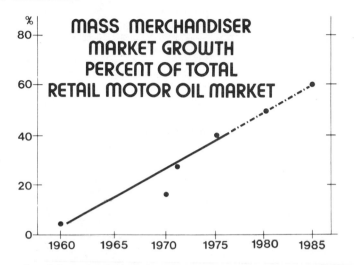

MASS MERCHANDISER MARKET GROWTH PERCENT OF TOTAL RETAIL MOTOR OIL MARKET

Special emphasis is being given sales to the mass merchandiser market which constitutes some 40 percent of total retail automotive oil sales. It is projected to increase to near 60 percent before it levels off in the 1980s.

We have initiated participation in trade shows to penetrate the mass merchandiser market. At our first show, we had some 3,500 registrations, and were able to write some 150,000 gallons of business.

Our mass merchandiser program, underway about six months, has been encouraging. At one New Jersey chain of stores we have realized sales in excess of 350,000 gallons where none existed prior to our program. We have introduced new container design and simplified instructions for the do-it-yourselfer.

We view TBA sales as an excellent opportunity to supplement profits from Company products. In 1976 we sold some $41 million worth of TBA; 114 percent over 1971. Presently we have an outstanding list of suppliers, and efforts to expand on this base are being conducted. TBA is a very valuable business and greatly complements other Division product sales.

Our market is highly competitive and it will take some time for lubricants to reach their true market values. We are quite optimistic about the future. We have a lean operation, made up of highly competent personnel and are in place to make a profit.

Retail Marketing

Our basic objective is: To market gasoline and merchandise and/or services, to satisfy the consumers' demand for convenience and value, through profit centered retail facilities utilizing innovative retail concepts and techniques consistent with sound financial management. Operating methods and techniques will be employed which allow the division to compete successfully in the retail marketplace.

Retail Marketing

The strategies employed are: 1) Reduce the investment per outlet and the total invested capital utilized in retail marketing. 2) Achieve maximum operating efficiencies that allow us to compete successfully. 3) Use self-service retailing wherever possible. 4) Seek other revenues to replace automotive mechanical service. This particular strategy has become increasingly important in the highly competitive retail gasoline market. In 1971, we tested and found that the retailing of convenience merchandise, along with gasoline, enhanced revenue potential and the resultant return on assets.

Our objective is to select that type of facility that will best meet local consumer needs and to give the Company the best overall volume and profit operation. In most cases, the self-service, Quik Mart, salary operation is the best retail unit. However, there are other areas that are better served through dealer-operated, full-service type facilities. A dealer program is being maintained for continuing some dealer-operated stations.

While we have been involved with developing and implementing new strategies, we have continually observed competitive activity.

Additionally, we examine segments of the industry data base for trends as they develop. Gasoline demand has shown a strong comeback from the embargo days and the economic recession that followed. We do not expect sustained growth of the current magnitude indefinitely into the future. There are two main reasons we foresee a leveling off as we approach 1985. First is the legislated miles per gallon minimum

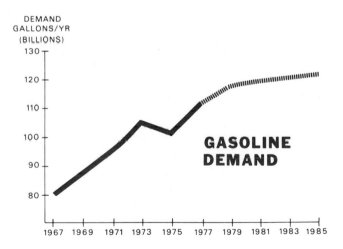

that becomes effective in 1978. Second is that the declining birth rate begins to be felt in the driving age population about 1985. Within this demand we have three opportunities for growth: 1) Growth in raw demand, 2) growth in geographic relocation, and 3) growth associated with the new concepts replacing old.

We have stated that an increase in the unit volume of salary-operated, lessee-dealer and management fee service stations would be forthcoming. Unit volume for these categories of retail outlets averages about 45,000 gallons per month while the industry average is near 34,000 gallons per month.

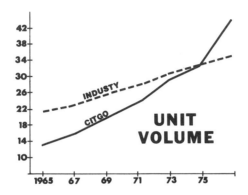

Market shares started showing noticeable erosion from the "major" sector to the "independents" in the 1960s and the trend continues. Portions of several "majors" are marketing as "independents" and we estimate that the "independent" marketing concept may account for 45 - 50 percent of the gasoline currently being retailed. It is not uncommon for the "independent" gasoline retailer to have unit volume averages of 125,000 - 165,000 gallons per month, approximately the same as our CITGO Quik Marts. One of the results of the change in industry unit volume is and will be the reduction in numbers of gasoline service stations. The number of service stations peaked at nearly 220,000 in 1969 and is expected to drop to the 135,000 level near 1980. Something near that number should be the leveling off point.

We have divided ourselves into five marketing areas with headquarters near Miami, Washington, Boston, Chicago, and New York. Since restructuring our retail marketing concepts in 1972, a lot of progress has been made. The number of operating units has been reduced by more than 50 percent, while at the same time retaining 80 percent of the volume. The service station investment base is expected to drop nearly $100 million from 1972 while total volume is expected to increase some 240 million gallons. Total gasoline sales will approach 1 billion gallons annually.

Our Chicago market is about the largest single grouping of stations we have planned for restructuring and it is expected to be completed in 1977. We expect the number of operating facilities to be reduced from 237 to 59, the gross book investment reduced from $18 million to $10 million, and a substantial increase in volume.

Older types of structures have been replaced by the Quik Mart facilities where the store is on the pump island. As conventional service stations, two units sold 40,000 gallons per month, each. After rebuilding, gasoline sales have increased to 206,000 and 160,000, respectively. Food sales per store are averaging $10,000 per month. We also have retail stores with the pump islands and store separated. Before rebuilding, two locations generated gasoline sales of 25,000 gallons each per month. Today volume has increased to 150,000 and 120,000, respectively. Food sales on a unit basis are averaging $8,000 per month.

With the increased numbers of stores, Quik Mart is achieving a brand identity all its own.

We believe our early decision to shift drastically our strategy is becoming increasingly important as it places us in a position to exploit the opportunities of a rapidly changing marketplace. All of the industry data and the observed actions of our competition lend support to our basic marketing concepts.

Earnings for 1976 were not adequate nor will they be in 1977. There are two fundamental reasons for this: First, is that the financial impact of restructuring a large asset base for another use is substantial; second, anytime marketing techniques and concepts undergo dramatic changes such as now taking place, a certain amount of chaos results and pricing actions frequently reflect the desire for volume as opposed to earnings. We believe time and maturity will correct both of these conditions.

We are proud of the changes we have been able to make since 1972, considering the governmental obstacles and the magnitude of the project. While we have set 1979 as the concluding date for the restructuring process, it is important that we search for ways to complete the changes at the earliest possible date.

<u>Supply and Transportation</u>

Cities Service has an interest in more than 18,000 miles of crude oil and refined products pipelines and has a 50 percent interest in a Company owning and operating fleet of 15 ocean-going tankers and 81 tugs and barges. The Company's supply and products distribution network is acknowledged to be one of our most important assets. Over the years, we have developed an efficient and economical petroleum transportation network by taking the initiative and aggressively promoting "industry" pipeline systems compatible with our requirements.

The Company's first venture in the pipeline business was in 1916 when a system was built to gather crude from the fields being developed in Kansas and Oklahoma. The first jointly owned pipeline system was the Texaco-Cities Service Pipe Line Company, founded in 1928. At that time, Cities Service was planning a crude oil pipeline from Oklahoma to serve the then new East Chicago refinery. It was learned that Texaco also was planning a small crude line to the Chicago area. By combining the requirements of both companies into a larger diameter line, significant operating efficiencies and economies of scale were realized.

Gradually over the years we have added to the crude pipeline network so that today we have an efficient, well-situated system that complements our refinery at Lake Charles.

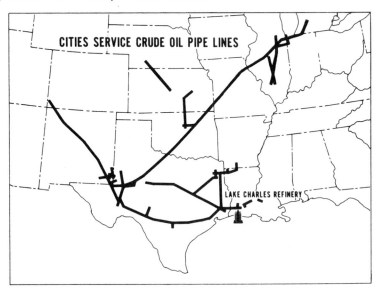

CITIES SERVICE CRUDE OIL PIPE LINES

LAKE CHARLES REFINERY

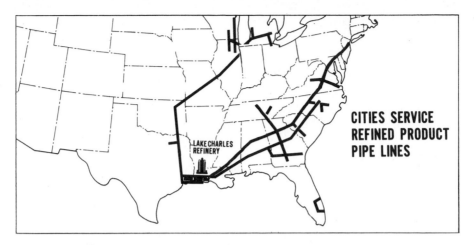

CITIES SERVICE
REFINED PRODUCT
PIPE LINES

The Company's participation in products distribution pipelines began with Wolverine Pipe Line Company in 1952. We have developed an efficient transportation system that approximately matches the Company's marketing territory.

We have always been a leader in the development of joint venture pipeline systems. This is best exemplified by Colonial Pipeline, the world's largest and most successful products system. Cities Service conceived the project and was instrumental in its development. Colonial became operational in 1963, and after six major expansions, consists of 4,200 miles of pipeline. This year, it will transport about 1.7 million barrels per day of products--or one out of every seven gallons of gasoline and light fuel oils consumed in the U.S. We receive products through 36 terminals on the Colonial system.

Explorer Pipeline was placed in service in 1971. It ties Lake Charles directly into our midwestern products system via a large terminal, which was developed at East Chicago when the refinery was shut down. Barges and tankers supplement the pipeline system by transporting products from Lake Charles directly to coastal markets in Florida, the South Atlantic and New England.

Thus, with our refinery at an ideal point for receiving crude and a well-conceived network for distributing products to its customers, the Company has a logistics system which results in a very competitive total transportation cost.

Our marine support activities include operation of a crude oil port and terminal just south of the Lake Charles refinery on the Calcasieu River.

Our utilization of large tankers is through the use of a transship-ment terminal on the Netherland Antilles Island of Bonaire, located off the coast of Venezuela. Here crude oil is transferred from supertankers into tankage and then reloaded into smaller vessels for delivery to Lake Charles. The increasing requirements for imported crude oil, and the well-publicized hazards associated with small tanker movements to coastal refineries, clearly indicate the growing need for offshore deep-water ports.

In recent years, we have concentrated our efforts on the SEADOCK project--a deepwater crude oil port to be located in the Gulf of Mexico near Freeport, Texas. It must be built 26 miles offshore in order to be in a water depth that will accommodate large tankers. The

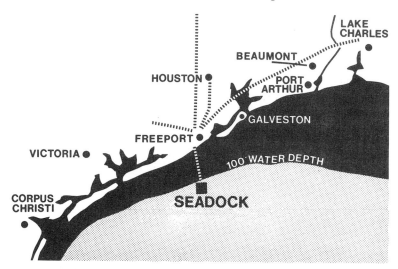

feasibility study of this project was initiated in 1972 by Cities Ser-vice and two other companies. Presently, the nine SEADOCK owners are evaluating whether or not they can prudently move ahead with the project in view of burdensome conditions incorporated into the license that was granted by the Federal Government in early 1977. We are hopeful that SEADOCK will become a reality and provide a far more efficient and environmentally acceptable method of receiving the na-tion's necessary imports of crude oil.

The U.S. is experiencing a dramatic change in the logistics of its crude oil supply. A significant redistribution is occuring because of the phaseout of Canadian crude supplies to Northern U.S. refineries. This, coupled with the imminent availability of Alaskan oil, has spawned interest in a new pipeline network from the Pacific Coast to the Midwest and, possibly even to Gulf Coast refining centers or across Central America.

There has been dramatic growth in the volume handled by the pipeline systems in which we have an ownership. It is apparent that the Company has been fortunate in having people who recognized the importance of efficient, low-cost petroleum transportation--and who were willing to provide the leadership to develop the country's system.

CITIES SERVICE PIPELINE SYSTEMS

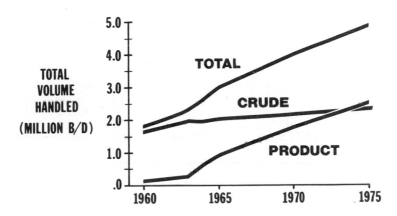

Cities Service conceived and promoted many of the significant transportation developments--the first joint interest pipeline, Colonial, Explorer, and now SEADOCK. We are dedicated to continuing this leadership role.

Wholesale Marketing and Refining

The Lake Charles refinery broke all previous records in crude runs, total throughput, and gasoline production in 1976. Crude runs averaged just over 250,000 barrels per day, natural gas liquids about 15,000 barrels per day, and purchased oils (mainly cat-cracker feed) about 14,000 barrels per day for a total input of just under 280,000 barrels per day.

1976–LAKE CHARLES REFINERY OPERATION

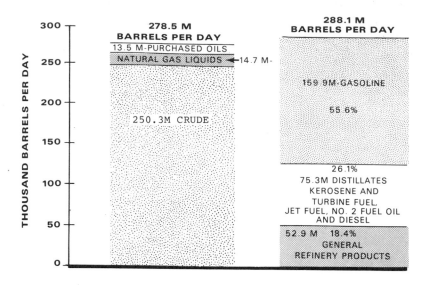

Lake Charles is one of the highest conversion refineries in the world. Gasoline production averaged almost 160,000 barrels per day, 64 percent based on crude. In comparison, gasoline production for all U.S. refineries was 57 percent based on crude. Total distillate production was over 75,000 barrels per day. Other refinery products amounted to about 53,000 barrels per day of which 9,000 barrels per day were liquid fuels burned in the complex. Total refinery production, then, amounted to just over 288,000 barrels per day.

Our refinery capacity is limited by bottom of the barrel handling capability. At high crude runs, we are forced to make more No. 6 fuel oil than we need for fuel. Since No. 6 prices historically have been below incremental crude cost, continuous sale of this product has not been attractive. However, by maximizing our cat-cracking capacity, this problem was partially solved in 1976 by charging 15,000 barrels per day of this residium to the three cat-crackers, and converting it to gasoline and No. 2 fuel oil. Residium cracking has been practiced only to a limited extent by the refining industry, and we consider this to be a highly successful innovation.

In 1972, our crude runs were essentially all domestic. Our imports of foreign crude have increased each year since 1972, and amounted to 63,000 barrels per day or 25 percent in 1976. The 1976 imports were essentially all sweet crudes. We plan to increase our sour crude processing capability by 25,000 barrels per day later this year, thus increasing the percentage of sour crude in our crude slate.

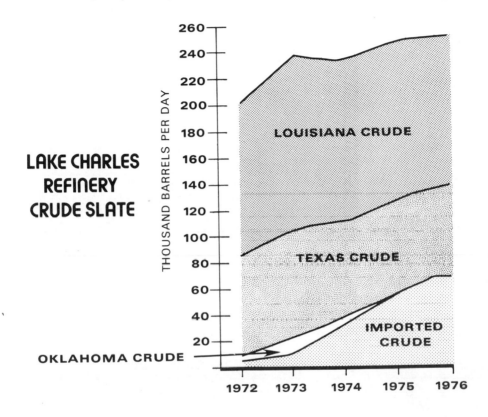

The Supreme Court ruled in June 1976 that the Environmental Protection Agency had the authority to phase down lead additives in gasoline. The present EPA schedule calls for a reduction to 0.8 gram per gallon after January 1, 1978, and down to 0.5 gram per gallon after October 1, 1979. This creates a double-barrelled downward effect on our gasoline production.

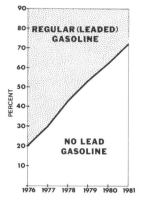

**PROJECTED
NO LEAD
GASOLINE
DEMAND**

Increasing volumes of lead-free gasoline require a higher refinery gasoline pool octane. When octane producing units have reached their capacity, pool octane is improved by rejecting lower octane components thereby reducing total gasoline production. When the use of lead to boost octane of gasoline components is restricted, components such as purchased raw naphthas, natural gasoline, and raffinates have to be rejected; thus, gasoline production is further reduced. Manganese is a new additive we began using in late 1976 to boost the octane of our no-lead gasoline. The alternative, of course, to reduced gasoline, is to build additional reforming capacity. The economics and costs of this additional capacity are being developed.

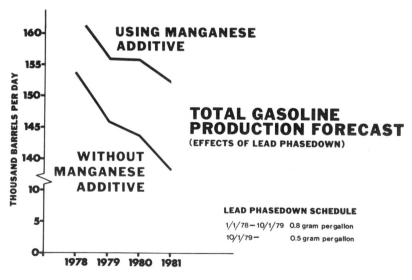

For some time, we have had a major fuel conservation program under way. Based on total throughput, our energy consumption at the refinery dropped 22 percent from 1972 through 1976, equivalent to 7,084 barrels of oil daily.

The major portion of our 1977 capital expenditure program at the refinery is directed toward the three following areas: continuation of our energy conservation program; limited crude expansion; and major automation for process control.

We have approached the costly problem of crude expansion cautiously. But we do have excellent economics on a small crude expansion of 22,000 barrels per day which can be accomplished by revamping an idle tower and furnace at the hydroformer.

The first phase of our automation project will enable us to operate two large crude topping units, the three cat-crackers, and the Gas Recovery Unit from a central control room by computer control. The ultimate goal of the project is to control by computer the entire refinery from one or possibly two locations.

The Wholesale Marketing unit is charged with the responsibility to market, at maximum net backs, a substantial portion of the light oil yield of the Lake Charles refinery. This is done with a field sales group of 35 people placed strategically through our marketing territory without the need for real estate investment beyond our transportation and distribution system.

We market about 3.25 billion gallons of gasoline, distillates, and aviation fuels with a marketing cost of only six-hundredths of a cent per gallon.

This low cost of marketing is achieved to a considerable degree because we sell our products to marketer/resellers or industrial consumers and airlines f.o.b. our terminals at a "rack price" with no further marketing expense except identification and minor brand support costs for branded distributors with their own marketing facilities. The ultimate market plan is to maintain relations only with those key branded distributors whose marketing philosophy is in concert with ours. These will be distributors who can thrive in the highly competitive marketplace utilizing innovative marketing styles--self-service, convenience items--the independent approach.

In addition to those marketing under the CITGO brand, a substantial part of our business includes the sale of 837 million gallons annually of gasoline to unbranded distributors. It is our plan to continue to supply a few unbranded distributors.

We have another sizeable business segment in turbine and jet fuel where sales exceed 300 million gallons annually. We have about 50 percent of the Florida "Gold Coast" aviation fuel business in the Miami, Fort Lauderdale, and West Palm Beach airports. Additionally, the Federal Government buys about 40 million gallons of JP-4 fuel from us annually.

We are beginning to enter an emerging market for No. 2 fuel oil to industrial consumers with year-round demands because of natural gas interruptions. These sales are primarily to utilities and large manufacturers by barge, pipeline tender, and cargo.

II. PROCEDURES AND REQUESTS FOR INFORMATION

Written operational procedures are valuable, if
not essential, documents for all businesses. If they
are well-conceived, clearly written, and faithfully
followed, procedures can help businesses achieve
higher levels of consistency, accuracy, quality, fair-
ness, and efficiency. They can vary greatly in com-
plexity and purpose--from simple procedures for emergency evacuation of a building to procedures for shutting down a nuclear reactor; from instructions on how
to fill out a personal information form to the procedures to follow in evaluating the efficiency of a manufacturing plant.

While most procedures are documents used for constant reference and therefore can be corrected as the
problems become apparent, many others are included in
special, one-time requests for information and must
consequently be scrutinized especially carefully to
ensure that the information returned will be consistent from response to response. The request itself
should not only present a clear procedure but also
provide the employee understandable reasons for the
request. People always want to know "why" they are
asked to do anything.

This section contains two examples of requests
that contain procedures for employees to follow and
one example of a standing procedure.

II. PROCEDURES AND REQUESTS FOR INFORMATION

    6.   Security Analysts--Sales

        (The Chesapeake Corporation of Virginia)

THE COMPANY: With headquarters in West Point, Virginia, The Chesapeake Corporation of Virginia produces a wide variety of wood products including lumber, plywood, pulp, paper, and paper and corrugated containers. It employs 2,150 people.

THE REPORT: This report is a request for updated sales information and sales projections. It contains a procedure to facilitate the response of the managers involved. The information will be used to better inform security analysts (in this case Standard and Poor's) about the company's potential for investors.

THE CHESAPEAKE CORPORATION OF VIRGINIA

(INTER-OFFICE CORRESPONDENCE)

	G. W. Redd N. O. Lorensen	
TO:	R. D. Harrison S. J. Ryczak	**DATE:** August 16, 1977
IN RE:	Security Analysts - Sales	**FROM:** D. S. Baird

This fall we are undertaking a program to better inform Security Analysts of Chesapeake's potential as an investment. Mr. Olsson and Mr. Camp are making presentations to a group in Richmond. They will need information from us. Unfortunately, I will be away the month of September, so most of the work must be done by the indivuduals involved in each marketing product. You need to do two things:

1. Referring to the attached copy of my May 22, 1975 presentation to Standard and Poor's, take your area of responsibility and bring it up to date through the first eight months of this year. You may have to estimate August shipments.

2. Prepare a price history 1972 actual through August 1977, and then make a very careful estimate of how you think prices will perform from then through 1980. In the case of linerboard, use as a basis 42# market price. In years gone by, average the market price for those years. That means before freight and discounts, not mill net. In the paper area, use 50# multiwall, 57# grocery bag and 50# converting. For pulp, use only bleached hardwood. For export, use the most common grade basis weight of linerboard and bleached hardwood pulp. In addition, prepare a corresponding list of actual freight through August 1977 for each year, and an estimate of what the freight will be between now and the end of 1980.

This research must be careful and factual. The years through 1980 must be your most honest opinion. Security Analysts, when fed any item of misinformation, can turn sour on a company forever. Tell it as it is, without embellishments. In that a lot of preparation will go into this program, including the making of slides and charts, this portion will have to be given to Carter Fox before September 15. Channel it through George Redd, who will have to summarize the total mill breakdown.

D. S. Baird

DSB:dnm

cc: J. C. Fox

II.   PROCEDURES AND REQUESTS FOR INFORMATION

    7.   Office Systems--Intra-Company
            Telephone Charge Study

         (Equifax Corporation)

THE COMPANY: Located in Atlanta, Georgia, Equifax pro-
                    vides services to businesses in three
                    areas: Risk Management (informational
                    services enabling employees, insurers,
                    and self-insurers to select and evaluate
                    business risks), Financial Control (infor-
                    mational and administrative services to
                    help businesses manage their assets), and
                    General Business (administrative systems,
                    market research, etc.). The company em-
                    ploys 12,966 people.

THE REPORT: This report outlines the procedure that
                    must be followed for Equifax to make an
                    in-house study of its intra-company tele-
                    phone charges. The success of the study
                    and thus the value of the analytical re-
                    port it will generate depend in large
                    measure on this report being clear and
                    effective.

MEMORANDUM

TO .... Managers, Sub-offices, & Sales Points (U. S. Only)

FROM .... Systems Design Unit

SUBJECT ...... OFFICE SYSTEMS - INTRA-COMPANY TELEPHONE CHARGE STUDY

DATE 8/22/77

RE CORRES ...   COPY TO ...

Systems Design Unit is currently studying the effect that non-customer chargeable intra-company telephone charges have on the cost of various reports and their profit contribution. At this point in the study, your input is needed.

1. Please contact your local telephone represen-tative and determine your next full billing period. This is the time between your upcoming cut-off date and the following cut-off date.

2. During the next full billing period insure that a Tel & Tel Expense Form 149-R is thoroughly completed on EVERY intra-company long distance call for which you <u>cannot</u> charge a customer. This should include <u>message</u> unit charges also.

3. Match the 149-R forms with the telephone bill when it arrives and compute the "Cost of Tel or Tel", showing total Telephone Company charge plus taxes. <u>No</u> surcharge is added to intra-company calls.

4. Assign someone in your office the responsibility to check each form to be sent to the Home Office for completeness. Critical areas are Type Report(s), Explanation & Cost of Tel or Tel. (see sample

(Over)

Equifax Services Inc.
Equifax Services Ltd.
Form 104—2-77 U.S.A.

of Form 149-R below).

```
┌─────────────────────────────────────────────────────────────────────────────┐
│                              ★ FILL OUT ONLY ACCOUNT NUMBER AND CASE NAME      │
│                                IF THIS FORM IS SUBMITTED WITH AN INQUIRY.      │
│                                OTHERWISE COMPLETE ENTIRE LD. SECTION.          │
│ ☐ CUSTOMER TELEGRAPH EXPENSE (90)    ★ ACCT. NO.____  —                        │
│   (SEND TO H.O. IN PACKAGE OF BUSINESS)  DATE TODAY      : 8-2-77              │
│ ☒ INTRA-COMPANY T.&T. (90)           NAME OF PERSON REQ. : J. SMITH           │
│   (NOT CHARGEABLE TO CUSTOMER. SEND TO   EQUIFAX INC.                          │
│   H.O. ACCOUNTING DEPT. WITH MONTHLY     OR CUSTOMER                           │
│   TELEPHONE OR TELEGRAPH STATEMENT)   DIST., AGCY., BRANCH : ____  —           │
│   TYPE OF REPORT (BE SPECIFIC)       FILE. POL., CLAIM NO. : 45D69F            │
│ ★ LIFE PERSONAL                      EQUIFAX INC. B.O. OR                       │
│                                      SALES POINT          : ATLANTA           │
│                                      SPECIAL BILLING IDENTIFICATION :          │
│ CASE                                                                           │
│ NAME :   FANNIG              MARY          J.                                  │
│          (Last)            (First)    (Middle Initial)                         │
│                                                                               │
│   To JACKSONVILLE, FLA                      ┌──────────────┐                   │
│         (City or Destination)               │  Cost of     │                   │
│                                             │ Tel. or Tel. │                   │
│   From ATLANTA                              │  ★           │                   │
│         (Branch Office or Sales Point)      │              │                   │
│ ★ EXPLANATION                               │              │                   │
│   TRACING REPORT ORDERED 7/5/77             │   $1.42      │                   │
│                                             │              │                   │
│   B.O. or Sales Authorization  JEH          └──────────────┘                   │
│                                    (Initials)                                  │
│ 149-R-1-76                                                                     │
└─────────────────────────────────────────────────────────────────────────────┘
```

* CRITICAL AREAS - MUST BE COMPLETED ON EACH FORM

    If more than one report was discussed during a
single call, show type and number of each. (For
example, Life-2, Auto-1).

5. Mail all 149-R forms for intra-company calls
   along with your telephone bill including the long
   distance charge portion to the Home Office,
   Systems Design. We will forward to Accounting,
   Department in time for regular processing.

For this study to be meaningful, one hundred percent accurate
response is imperative. Thanks for your cooperation.

II. PROCEDURES AND REQUESTS FOR INFORMATION

8.   Shoplifting Policies and Procedures

(Bruno's Food Stores, Inc.)

THE COMPANY: Bruno's Food Stores, Inc., owns and oper-
                ates a chain of retail supermarkets in
                Alabama. Company headquarters are located
                in Birmingham, Alabama.

THE REPORT: This report presents Bruno's policies and
                procedures designed to prevent shoplifting.
                In order to be effective, these procedures
                must be detailed enough to ensure employees
                will stay within the limits of the law as
                they protect the interests of the store, and
                yet the procedures must be simple and clear
                enough to allow employees to read and re-
                view them quickly.

BRUNO'S INC.

SHOPLIFTING POLICIES AND PROCEDURES

All employees have responsibility in the detection, apprehension and prosecution
of shoplifters. Therefore, all employees must have a clear understanding
of the action to be taken when a shoplifter is discovered. Store managers,
especially, must be well acquainted with the procedures contained herein. These
procedures also apply to any person employed for the purpose of containing shoplifting, whether employed individually, or through a security service.

PURPOSE

To discourage shoplifters from stealing in our stores and to reduce the loss for
which they are accountable.

POLICY

Detection, arrest, and prosecution are an effective deterrent to shoplifting.
To support a charge of shoplifting and obtain a conviction the deterrent is only
effective when the methods employed prior to, during and after the apprehension
are legally proper and adequate to produce sufficient evidence.

PROCEDURE

    A. Detection

        1. When an actual concealment of merchandise has been witnessed, keep the
            shoplifter under constant observation, concentrating on the location of
            the stolen goods and the type of merchandise involved.

        2. Attract the attention of another employee to serve as a witness to the
            apprehension and recovery of the merchandise.

        3. Alert a member of the management for the purpose of making the apprehension.

    B. Apprehension

        1. The management representative should confront the shoplifter only when
            positive that:

            a. The shoplifter took the merchandise.

            b. The merchandise is still in the shoplifter's possession.

            c. The shoplifter has checked out, or otherwise passes the check out
               counter.

PROCEDURE (continued)

B. Apprehension

    2. The management representative, in the presence of another employee, will address the shoplifter by saying, "Excuse me, there is a private matter I would like to discuss with you in the store office." Never accuse the shoplifter of stealing or use the words "thief" or "steal". Never indicate that a "mistake" has been made.

    3. In the process of directing the shoplifter to return to the store:

        a. Never use force.

        b. Never touch the shoplifter.

        c. Never threaten to call the police if the shoplifter refuses to accompany you into the store.

        d. If the shoplifter refuses to return to the store, let him or her leave. Report the incident to the Security Department and the local police.

    4. Have another employee, along with management's representative, accompany the shoplifter to a location in the store, out of public view and earshot. If the shoplifter is a female, the other employee must be a female.

    5. When the shoplifter, management representative, and employee-witness reach the place selected for the interview, request return of merchandise. Pay particular attention to the place of concealment, but do not search the person or personal effects of the shoplifter.

    6. If the shoplifter no longer has the concealed merchandise, let him or her leave. Report the incident to the Security Department promptly.

C. Interview

    1. Without threats or promises, attempt to obtain a statement from the shoplifter using the sample form in this section. In so doing, exercise care in establishing the shoplifter's identity and address by checking driver's license, social security card, or other means of identification. Be sure the person signs the form on the proper line.

    2. Obtain separate, written statement from witnesses in the event the shoplifter refuses to sign. Include shoplifter's oral admission in the witness statement.

    3. Never accept payment for the stolen merchandise.

D. Prosecuting the Case

    1. The merchandise stolen by the shoplifter will be marked for identification by the management representative and the employee-witness so that it can be positively recognized at the trial. Identification will consist of initials, date, store location, and shoplifter's name.

PROCEDURE (continued)

D. Prosecuting the Case

    2. Complete the "Shoplifting Incident Report". This information will be used to guide the prosecuting attorney and the security department.

    3. Summon the local police.

        a. Place a call to the police out of the hearing of the shoplifter.

        b. Provide them with details of the offense.

        c. If the shoplifter is a juvenile, turn the juvenile over to the police and rely upon the police to decide the disposition of the case.

        d. Agree to sign an affidavit charging the shoplifter with a criminal charge. Do not sign, however, if the prosecuting attorney advises against it.

        e. Release the merchandise marked for identification to the police and obtain a receipt. If the police refuse to accept it, safeguard the merchandise until the trial and be prepared to show continuity of possession. Retain the merchandise and if perishable, photograph or freeze it.

        f. Release to the prosecuting attorney, if he so desires, a copy of the shoplifter's statement and the incident report.

E. Court Appearance

    1. It is of utmost importance that management's representative and the employee-witness appear in court to testify against the shoplifter. The effectiveness of their testimony will depend upon:

        a. A neat, business-like appearance.

        b. Thorough knowledge of the facts attendant to the offense.

        c. Recitiation of the facts in a composed and impartial manner.

        d. An ability to listen and understand the question before answering.

        e. The truth of the witness.

F. Disposition

Immediately upon completion of the "Shoplifting Incident Report", forward a copy to the Security Department. Attach other pertinent documents, if any. Complete file is to be retained for three (3) years after the incident.

G. Reports

The "Shoplifting Incident Reports" are extremely important. A report must be completed each time a person is stopped. Additionally, it is equally important to complete a report when a person is not prosecuted as when a prosecution is completed. Each report must be completed in full and store stamped in some way.

HINTS FOR DETECTING SHOPLIFTERS

Watch for customers who hang around and handle items and make no attempt to buy anything.

Watch for the customer who has luggage, briefcase of other large items.

Look out for acts that distract the clerk while an accomplice does the stealing.

Watch for purses, oversize handbags, open packages or shopping bags carried or in bascarts.

Be careful of the customer who is nervous when he picks up merchandise - he may buy it or steal it.

Watch people who hang around the displays which are hidden from clerks.

Watch for people who wear heavy clothing in mild weather.

Watch for children and teenagers when they are grouped around displays.

Watch for the customer who seems to be waiting for someone or maybe watching for someone to show up.

Watch for the person who keeps walking around and buys nothing.

Always be careful of the person who always has a handkerchief or gloves in her hand and handles merchandise in the same hand.

Be careful of people going into receiving rooms or stock rooms who have no business in these places.

Watch for the customer who, upon entering the store, takes her wallet out of her purse and holds the wallet in her hand. (This eliminates need to open purse at checkstand).

SUMMARY

	DO		DON'T

DO

1. When you see a subject conceal merchandise, <u>keep him or her in sight at all times</u>.

2. Have another employee accompany you when you approach subject. State that you would like to discuss a private matter in the store office.

3. If it is determined that subject was not shoplifting, apologize, explain why the inquiry was made, and let the subject go.

4. If the person was shoplifting, get a written statement, get and keep the goods, call the police, and sign a warrant if requested.

5. After arrest has been made, write down what happened and obtain a similar report from employee-witness.

DON'T

1. Don't approach subject until he has passed the checkout counter.

2. Don't use the words "steal" "thief" or "mistake" or words of like import. Don't hold subject physically. Don't promise not to have subject arrested or prosecuted.

3. Don't search the subject.

4. Don't discuss the matter with anyone but your superiors and the police.

5. Don't agree to drop prosecution or make any deal with the subject.

APPREHENSION (attachment)

These elements are to be followed in All Shoplifting apprehensions:

1. The person who will apprehend the shoplifter must see the suspect conceal the merchandise.

2. This same person must know exactly what the merchandise is.

3. In addition, this same person must know where the merchandise is concealed.

4. After seeing the merchandise concealed, the suspect must be kept under constant surveillance.

5. The suspect MUST be allowed to pass through the check lanes. (Even though certain laws state that concealment is enough to justify apprehension for shoplifting, our policy is very rigid in requiring that suspect pass through the check lanes prior to apprehension.)

6. If, after apprehension, it is determined that a criminal warrant will be obtained, it is mandatory that the individual who saw the crime committed personally sign the criminal warrant. (Subject to local policies)

If the above elements cannot be met in each shoplifting apprehension involving criminal prosecution, the employees involved and Bruno's itself face possible civil action. These steps are for your protection and they should be covered with all employees.

III. PROBLEM SOLVING REPORTS

Managers are constantly confronted with problems that must be solved to ensure a company's smooth operation or, in some cases, to ensure the company can continue to operate at all. Although the problems may vary greatly in magnitude, the report writer must follow the same basic procedure. He or she must analyze the problem, find and evaluate the alternative solutions, and then determine which of those possible solutions is best. Finally, the writer must produce a report which justifies his or her solution and provides whatever information the reader needs to understand the problem and the reasons for rejecting key alternatives.

In this section you will find reports that illustrate various ways of writing reports which solve (or explain solutions to) distinctly different problems.

III. PROBLEM SOLVING REPORTS

9. Final Destination Labeling on Air Cargo

(Delta Air Lines)

THE COMPANY: Delta Air Lines provides air transportation services for many U.S. and some foreign cities. Company headquarters are located in Atlanta, Georgia. Delta employs approximately 35,700 people.

THE REPORT: In large companies with high volumes of business, seemingly minor matters often demand careful attention. This report illustrates the close scrutiny managers at Delta Air Lines must give to details as small as destination labels on air freight packages.

(FOR INTRACOMPANY   CORRESPONDENCE ONLY)

DELTA
AIR LINES

DATE: December 16, 1976

TO: Vice President - Stations

FROM: Supervisor - Methods   PHONE:

SUBJECT: Final Destination Labeling on Air Cargo

As requested, Analysts Brown and McLaurin have investigated the alternatives for enlarging and clarifying the final destination codes on air cargo handled on the automated sortation system at the Atlanta Air Cargo Terminal.

After observing the sortation operation at the air cargo terminal and consulting with supervision and personnel in this area and with Cargo Marketing and Stations management, four different proposals for clarifying the final destination code on packages were evaluated. These four alternatives are:

1) Revise the present Air Cargo Lot Label Stencil (Form 0412-90059) to enlarge the area for entering the destination code.

2) Have all stations sending air cargo through Atlanta apply a separate gum-backed destination label to each package (these labels must be moistened before applying to a package).

3) Have all stations apply a peel-off self-adhesive destination label to each package sent through Atlanta.

4) Have all stations apply a peel-off self-adhesive (or gum-backed) destination label to each package destined for the five or ten largest stations (by piece volume).

To evaluate each alternative, the cost of each approach and the ease of handling were determined. Based on records of Delta Air Cargo shipped in 1975, (12,053,080 pieces), the <u>additional</u> cost (material and forms only, not labor time for applying the additional gum-backed or self-adhesive labels) of providing each type label required would be:

	Revision of Present Lot Label	Gum-Backed Labels	Self-Adhesive Labels
Systemwide	$80.00	$29,981.06	$142,697.85
10 Largest (65% of system: ATL,ORD,DFW,MSY,MIA,DTW, BOS,LAX,MEM,IAH)	N/A	$19,187.88	$ 91,326.62
5 Largest (47% of system: ATL,DFW,ORD,MSY,MIA)	N/A	$14,091.10	$ 67,067.99

63

The costs for gum-backed and self-adhesive labels were determined after allowing for the packages which are received from air freight forwarders. These packages (approximately 32% of air cargo handled by Delta) are already labeled by destination when received.

Application of the gum-backed or self-adhesive labels would require additional time in preparing a package since the lot label would still be required. (This time is not included in the cost figures.)

Evaluation of the alternatives indicated that the most economical approach is to revise the present lot label to allow more room for a large final destination code (see sample of proposed revision attached). The proposed revision is permissible under Trade Practice Manual guidelines for the industry Form AC-6. The AC-6 may be used in lieu of the AC-7 (our current lot label format).

It is recommended that the $80.00 revision of the present lot label be implemented prior to implementing any of the other alternatives as this approach allows full systemwide evaluation at minimal cost.

Please advise us which of these approaches you desire implemented. We will process the change or new orders and submit form proofs for your approval.

The cooperation of Atlanta Air Cargo personnel during this evaluation was greatly appreciated. Please let us know if we can answer any questions.

D. M. Schmidt

D. M. Schmidt

DMS/jmm

cc: Assistant Vice-President - Personnel Administration

Attachment

DELTA AIR LINES, INC.

FINAL AIRPORT DESTINATION

AIRBILL NUMBER

006 —

TOTAL NO. PIECES IN SHIPMENT	TOTAL SHIPMENT WEIGHT	WEIGHT OF THIS PIECE

TO	VIA	REMARKS	
	DL		
		DATE	C.O.D.

DELTA AIR LINES, INC.

FINAL AIRPORT DESTINATION

AIRBILL NUMBER

006 —

REMARKS

	TO	VIA
		DL

Total No. Pieces In Shipment	Total Shipment Weight	Weight Of This Piece
DATE	C.O.D.	

III.   PROBLEM SOLVING REPORTS

    10.   "Fort Smith Gas Shortage"

    11.   "Report on Meeting at Homestead Valve"

              (Baldor Electric Company)

THE COMPANY: Located in Fort Smith, Arkansas, Baldor
                  Electric Company manufactures electric
                  motors, electric motor grinders, and
                  dental lathes. Baldor employs 2400 people.
                  Fred Ballman is Chairman of the company
                  and Roland S. Boreman, Jr. is President.

THE REPORTS: Report #10 summarizes the steps taken to
                  prevent the possible shutdown of a manu-
                  facturing plant due to a shortage of
                  natural gas. Report #11 records a meeting
                  between representatives of Baldor and
                  Homestead Valve, a client of Baldor; this
                  report not only presents Homestead's
                  compliments and complaints but also explains
                  what steps have been taken to eliminate the
                  problems the Homestead people pointed out.
                  Baldor Electric is small enough that its
                  managers can solve problems among themselves
                  without using reports as decision-making
                  tools. Therefore, the reports written
                  within this company are mainly records of
                  actions taken. What influence does this
                  situation have on the format and organiza-
                  tion of these reports?

FORT SMITH GAS SHORTAGE

Because of a purported gas shortage last winter (early 1976), our Fort Smith plant closed down for several days. It was an emergency measure and we were not as well informed as we might have been. The gas company has indicated publicly that they will probably be faced with a similar shortage again this coming winter. Accordingly, we have been in contact with Mr. Waelder, who is the Operations Manager of the Fort Smith Gas Company.

He stated that their rule last year did not actually require the closing of a plant, but rather, the discontinuation of all use of gas for processing. He stated that our plant could have continued to stay open and have full use of gas for the heaters and otherwise maintaining personnel comfort. However, we would have had to discontinue the use of all gas for our dip and bake oven and for our rotor casting room.

He stated that regardless of what we thought, that was their company regulation last year and will again be their company regulation this year if such a gas shortage should occur. Last year, we were curtailed one time for two days, but should the weather be more severe this year, we could be curtailed for longer periods and more than one time.

We were contemplating running a gas line from a nearby gas well and piping it in directly for our use. For several reasons, this has now become impractical and we will not consider this further at this time. It was also thought that if we could connect directly to the high-pressure gas line which cuts across our property, that we would not be subject to the local shutdown rule. We now have our furnace room directly connected to this high-pressure source. Mr. Waelder tells us that this is not the case, however, and that should we be curtailed again, that it will control our use of both the gas from the high-pressure main and also that from the low-pressure city mains.

Therefore, it is our decision to put in some limited standby supply of propane. We have investigated this and find that the propane will be no problem at all to obtain during non-peak use periods and perhaps even during other gas curtailments, so long as we have a prior arrangement made. I've talked with Bill about his Casting Department which is our biggest gas consumer, and he states that he could stand casting room shutdowns of several days occasionally throughout the year without drastically effecting his other production. He states further, however, that he could not stand for a shutdown of his dip and bake unit for more than 24 hours without shutting down our other production.

We have made an estimate of the gas usage of our dip and bake unit and designed standby equipment for two weeks operation. This will consist of 1000 gallon propane tank along with suitable valves and regulators for switching from natural gas to the propane gas when required. Changeover time would be a matter of minutes and consist simply of closing and opening certain valves and relighting the furnace. Estimate of the total cost of this equipment is less than $4,000. We have already instructed Roman to proceed with this equipment immediately and Purchasing should proceed with necessary arrangements to get the tank filled with propane and replenished when required.

Fred C. Ballman
Oct. 6, 1976

67

REPORT ON MEETING AT HOMESTEAD VALVE

This meeting was requested by Homestead Valve and took place at
their plant in Pittsburgh on August 10, 1976. Baldor was represented at this meeting by Ballman, Boreham, Gerding, and Fank-
hauser. Homestead's personnel at this meeting were Fred Schuchman,
President; Fred Kruger, Chief Engineer; Dick Sinclair, Purchasing
Agent; Rudy Radek, Quality Control Mgr; Russ Reisdorf; Leon Farbotnik.

Mr. Kruger conducted the meeting and started by stating Baldor
advantages to Homestead Valve:

  1. Most motor for the dollar.

  2. Most flexible for their changing needs.

  3. Most cooperation.

He followed this by saying that these advantages were not without certain problems. Again, there were three which later were
discussed in detail and was the real purpose for the meeting.
These areas were:

  1. Quality.

  2. Field service.

  3. Desired design changes.

The need for quality improvement was considered first. Mr. Kruger
mentioned that rejects sometimes ran as high as 7%. He stated
further that there were numerous miscellaneous problems, but
that two of them were so important as to warrant special corrective effort.

Improperly operated thermals in the past has been the most serious.
It was brought out that one of the Baldor specs called for the
wrong thermal which has now since been corrected. There have
been shop mistakes and even mistakes by Texas Instruments.
Mr. Kruger admitted that thermal operation lately has been better
but they still have some nuisance trips in the field. I asked
them to look for defective thermals and to try returning them
to me personally. I will then determine whether the thermal is
defective or mismarked, or whether Baldor made a mistake. Our
analysis can dictate a course of action. In the meantime, I will
have Engineering review and test if necessary the various windings
involved. We should search our files in the shop, in the computer,
and in Engineering for incorrect records. Again, I suggest Engineering give me a correct list and I will follow with a search of
the various files myself.

They were most disturbed by our switch problems. We have instituted
many improvements, but it seems that as fast as we cure one problem
at Homestead, another one crops up. The latest was sticking collars.
(We have already instituted corrections for this problem.)

It is already my intention to schedule a follow-up Q.I. meeting
on switches and we will place special emphasis on Homestead motors.

At about this point in our meeting, Mr. Schuchman brought up the
matter of our field service organization. He first complained
about lack of service in England and other countries. Rolly said
his remark was most timely since we were just now taking steps
to vastly improve our overseas service. Mr. Schuchman then pro-
ceeded to tell about the lack of cooperation with our home service,
particularly pointing out Canada. Rolly was displeased with this
report and said he would get after this immediately. He took
some data and agreed to work closely with Homestead to solve
this problem.

The final phase of the meeting considered possible design modifications. Leo complained about the readability of our new lead
numbers. He stated they were too small, faint and smudged with
paint. We have already eliminated the paint overspray. Rolly
stated that our next shipment of lead wire will be in a more con-
trasting color, 1" apart. Leo says that G.E. spacing is 1/2"
apart. Irregardless, I will instruct our shop to use the old
metal markers on all Homestead motors until we work out a marking
method to their satisfaction.

Leo next asked for a shaft change so as to give more usable shaft
length. This is a simple change and I will have Engineering make
a set of marked-up prints for their approval. It is so straight-
forward that we will immediately incorporate it in the 35 frame
but wait for their word on the other frames.

Leo next complained about the flimsy thermal cover. It does protect the thermal satisfactorily, but it is too easily dented. It
was suggested that we beef up our packaging but this wouldn't
please him as he still can dent it easily in his own shop handling.
We now make this cover of No. 20 gage. I will check the possibilities of changing to No. 60.

The final item was the elimination of the conduit box from the 35
frames. I explained that with our new terminal panel construction,
we could now make a simple stamping for housing the switch. They
seemed quite pleased with this news and wanted to go ahead. They
did point out that the spade connectors should be 1/4" wide which,
incidentally, is our standard.

We discussed the details of the stamping. The switch blister
should be moved in towards the shaft centerline of the motor as
far as possible. The toggle handle will project through the side
so as to extend radially at the side of the motor. The G.E. cover
was stamped "On" - "Off", which was very illegible. We will not
attempt to stamp directly into the cover itself but, rather,
supply our standard On-Off plate which we buy from the switch
manufacturer. We discussed the switch itself since we are to

furnish it and prewire it. They stated that they have no need for a switch on anything over 1 HP. However, since we will be able to use this scheme for other customers, we should study all of the 35 frame ratings and choose one or several switches which will cover the complete range. We should try real hard to use the switches that are already being used on our grinders. We will move this design project along quickly and I expect to have prints for their approval in the mail within the next few days.

Rolly will follow-up on the service problems and any other sales matters. I will follow-up on the engineering, tooling, quality and material items. I feel we are on the verge of becoming a satisfactory supplier and it behoves us to make special effort by both production and engineering. If we succeed in these two areas, we could easily become their major and perhaps only supplier.

Fred C. Ballman
August 16, 1976

III.   PROBLEM SOLVING REPORTS

   12.   Evaluation Board Review of Wood Operations Move

         (AMF Incorporated)

THE COMPANY: AMF Incorporated manufactures a wide range
                of products including sports equipment,
                sportswear, motorcycles, mopeds, industrial
                machinery, and timing devices. AMF's cor-
                porate headquarters are located in White
                Plains, New York. The company employs ap-
                proximately 28,000 people.

THE REPORT: The purpose of this report is to recommend
                and justify moving a manufacturing opera-
                tion (small electrical products) from Dan-
                vers, Massachusetts, to Gainsville, Geor-
                gia. The report illustrates the many dif-
                ferent but interrelated factors managers
                must take into account when contemplating
                such a move. Note that this report writer
                does present and evaluate rejected alter-
                natives to the Gainsville move to show that
                he had carefully considered several less
                radical solutions to the problems at Dan-
                vers.

71

INTEROFFICE CORRESPONDENCE

TO: S. Groner/E. M. Wastell   FROM: B. J. O'Connor

BUSINESS UNIT: BUSINESS UNIT:

LOCATION: LOCATION:

SUBJECT: Evaluation Board Review of   DATE: November 14, 1975
         Wood Operations Move

    At your direction we have reviewed the proposal presented by Mr. J. E.
Mulheim at a October 31, 1975 Special OMB, to relocate the Wood Electric
operation from Danvers, Mass., to the Potter & Brumfield plant in Gainesville
Georgia. To accomplish this task, we visited the Wood Operation on November
11, 1975, and discussed in detail with Mr. A. B. Davis, the Operations Manager,
those details pertinent to our review. It was unfortunate that due to the holiday
we were unable to observe the facility in production, but sifficient data was
generated from our discussions with which to complete the Wood segment of our
evaluation. We also visited, on 11/13/75, the Gainesville Georgia plant and
reviewed in detail, the financial and other back-up information provided by
J. Glass, P & B's Division Executive V.P.

    Our evaluation of this proposed relocation, will touch upon Manufacturing,
Financial, Engineering and Personnel aspects of the move. The latter two areas
will be analized in more detail in separate reports by Mr. Hosen and by the
Corporate Industrial Relations department.

WHY FILE THIS COPY?
    IF YOU MUST RETAIN THIS FOR REFERENCE, SPECIFY A DEFINITE RETENTION PERIOD:
    (SEE CORP PROC 11 2 FOR RETENTION SCHEDULE)
                  1 YEAR _____ OTHER _____

FORM 1 (REV. 7/69)

RECOMMENDATIONS

We recommend, based upon our review and analysis:

a)   That the Wood Electric manufacturing operations presently located
     at Danvers, Mass., be transferred to the P & B plant in Gainesville,
     Georgia.

b)   That P & B take whatever action is deemed necessary to insure the transfer
     of the four _essential_ Wood engineering staff members to Gainesville. Without
     this team, excessive delays in start up could occur, also serious sales and
     revenue losses could be experienced.

c)   That P & B seek to lease, nearby, temporary office space for "non-manufacturing"
     support personnel, and take other actions to insure _adequate_ office space for
     these "Wood" engineers and other critical personnel is available. We would
     also suggest P & B analize their _total_ space requirements at this facility in
     relation to their Strategic Plan revenue projections.

We support these recommendations based upon the following data:

A. Manufacturing

    o   The product, while containing a high level of engineering and quality input, requires average manufacturing skills.

    o   The process is basic assembly, easily transferred, easily learned. Manufacturing support equipment is basic, benches, test equipment, small tools, easily moved and re-set up.

B. Financial

    o   The present Danvers' Fixed costs can be reduced considerably through elimination of a portion of the Danvers' facility cost, a reduction in exempt, fixed salaries, medical departments, and other fixed expenses associated with an "independent" plant.

    o   Variable Overhead savings in non-duplicated functions as storerooms, material handlers, inspectors, maintenance and supplies are also possible.

    o   Savings in labor and material can be realized due to combined support functions as purchasing, accounting, tool room, etc.

    o   Capital expenditures for providing an alternate fuel supply, repairing various "facility" equipment and other capital expenses at Danvers can be avoided. ($110,000 planned in 1976).

    o   Difference in labor cost provides a savings if moved. ($4.27/hr Danvers versus $3.08/hr. Gainesville - Factored for efficiency).

    o   Some of the present Danvers' "fixed costs" (i.e., tool room) cannot support any additional revenue increases and must be expanded should sales accelerate.

o   Gross profits of over $2 million can be generated in the 1976–1978

    time period where $400,00 in loss would have occurred at Danvers

    for an investment of under $200,000.

C.   Engineering

We have found very little data concerning Engineering which would actually

support our recommendation. Most of our input is neutral or supports a

negative position. We do not believe , however, that the negative contrib-

utions are such that we should alter our recommendation.

o   If key engineers do not relocate several problems will occur:

    -   New product development will be delayed

    -   Revenue, derived from new products ($444,000 in 1977 and $884,000

        in 1978) could be delayed or lost.

o   Presently Gainesville has insufficient office space to accomodate key

    engineering people required for Wood Electric Products.

D.   Personnel

o   Gainesville presently has 50 skilled direct labor people on layoff.

o   No Union exists at Gainesville

o   Absenteeism at Gainesville is approximately 12% lower than Danvers.

    (15% Danvers vs. 3% Gainesville)

o   Incentive pay system provides a higher productivity level.

After reviewing the P & B proposal to the Special OMB, and our subsequent visits to Danvers and Gainesville, it became quite clear that Wood is having, and will continue to have problems in producing other than a "in the red" pretax profit unless some action is taken to change this course. There are several alternatives which could be considered, ranging from the most drastic, close the plant, to moving the plant completely. All have obvious social and financial implications.

P & B has chosen (quite obviously not the most drastic course of action, which would produce only negative results in both the social and financial planes), to consider moving the entire operation to a "sister" P & B plant. This decision reflecting the positive end of the scale.

Between these two opposing points lie a great many choices. We have reviewed some of these and offer them not so much as alternatives to P & B's chosen path, but as alternatives, which we analized and found not as attractive as the one preferred.

To repeat, between "close down", and move completely there are a multitude of various choices. A few of these are:

A.   What can be done to make Wood profitable without moving the operation?

    a) Drop unprofitable low activity lines and expand the profitable non-adjustable thermal line and others to include larger amp and fractional amp capacities.

    b) Reduce the cost of the product, to make it even more competitive and thus improve revenue.

Both of the preceeding are good logical techniques for putting Wood, Danvers in the "black". The Danvers' 6 man engineering staff has recently spawned four new engineering programs, one of which , the Mini-Mag relay, is now in the primary manufacturing stages, the other three should be at this same point within a year. With these four products, already anticipated in future revenue projections, the small Danvers' Engineering staff will be hard pressed to solve whatever problems remain in design, and still remain to be uncovered in manufacturing. Wood is not staffed to undertake a second product reduction/expansion at this time and if they were, the time lag from design to manufacture would probably not allow this type of project to produce revenue until 1978/1979.

To reduce the cost of the product would surely change the revenue requirement to "break even", but to do so, would also require Automation and mean large capital expenditures and engineering. We are not attempting to paint a completely black picture for Wood, but we are attempting to point out that the level of production which has been experienced at Wood, and that which is projected, is not sufficient to support the fixed costs inherent with the facility they occupy and the products themselves.

B. Move the Wood Electric operation to Vermont or New Hampshire and thus, enjoy the same benefits of low labor, low lease costs as experienced by R.C.L.

We sincerely doubt that if such a move was made, the union would not follow and organize at the new plant. Such a "follow" move would reduce considerably any Vermont/New Hampshire labor cost advantages, and might even threaten the presently envious position held by R.C.L.

Advantages to such a move would be, in addition to a "hoped" for labor cost advantage:

o   reduction in fixed cost contributed by lower facility expenses

o   a higher probability of retaining our key engineering & exempt people (virtually a "parallel" move)

This change would provide tangible savings in building costs, since some older mill type buildings in these areas (suitable for the Wood Manufacturing operation) lease for as low as $0.40/sq. ft. If we used $1.25 as an average cost, the 30,000 required square feet would cost $37,500/year, a potential savings of $32,700 over the present Wood lease. If we add taxes, etc., an estimated $40,000 in savings could conceivably result. This would change the 1976 Wood fixed from $777,000 to $737,000 and with some labor saving contributing an estimated variable profit pickup increase of 2%, we have: Note: See Product Line Analysis – P & B 1976 Budget.

From Exhibit A (in $000's)

	1976
Net Revenue	2,822
Cost of Sales	
Material	982
Labor	440
Variance 1	81
Var. O.H.	715
Fixed O.H.	737
Total C.O.S.	2,955
Gross Profits	(133)

The foregoing figures prove that it is volume and other Fixed Costs, not facility costs, which are hurting Wood. Thus, a move to another "non" P & B location is not feasible.

Other alternatives as moving parts of the product line, etc., are not reasonable since they do not address the prime cause of the Wood situation.

We have prepared P & L's for both Wood & Gainesville, which will show the impact of the transfer upon pretax profits. (See Exhibits A & B). Neither of these exhibits include G&A or other costs! Exhibit B, which depicts the impact on the Wood Operations, should the move to Gainesville be made, clearly shows that the combined savings in labor and total overheads projected by the move, make the operation profitable. Exhibit A, on the other hand, proves our point, that in the Danvers' location, Wood will not even be in a break-even position (at the Gross Profit level) in 1978.

EXHIBIT A

WOOD ELECTRIC – DANVERS
(in $000's)

	1975	1976	1977	1978
Net Revenue	1999 **	2822**	3731****	4674****
Cost of Sales				
Material @ 34.8% Rev.***	696	982	1298	1627
Labor @ 15.6% Rev.***	312	440	582	729
Variance @ 18.3% DL***	57	81	107	133
Var O.H. @ 162.5% DL***	507 @162.5%	715 @162.5%	946 @162.5%	1185
Fixed O.H. @ 206.7% DL***	645 @176.6%	777 @155.2%	903 @139.5%	1017
Total C.O.S.	2217	2995	3836	4691
Gross Profit	(218)	(173)	(105)	(17)

Fixed @ 206.7% = 645

$$\text{Fixed @ 206.7\%} = 645 \qquad @ 206.7\% = 909$$

$$\Delta \text{Fixed} = \frac{909-645}{2}$$

$$= 132$$

$$\frac{+ 645}{777}$$

$$@ 176.6\% = 1028$$

$$\Delta F = \frac{1028-777}{2}$$

$$= 126$$

$$\frac{+ 777}{903}$$

$$@ 155.2 = 1131$$

$$\Delta F = \frac{1131-903}{2}$$

$$= 114$$

$$\frac{+ 903}{1017}$$

Note: *We have constantly reduced the Fixed O.H. by 1/2 the difference in "past" year versus "next" year. This was done to factor the fixed for volume increases. We have not included any G&A or other expenses.

** See P & B 1976 Budget – Product Line Analysis

*** Per P & B backup information.

**** From 1976–1978 P & B Strategic Plan.

EXHIBIT B

WOOD ELECTRIC – GAINESVILLE
(in $000's)

	1975	1976	1977	1978
Net Revenue	1999*	2822	3731	4674
Cost of Sales				
Material @ 34.8% Rev***	–	982	1298	1627
Labor @ 72% Danvers ***	–	317	419	525
Variance @ 18.3% DL****	–	58	77	96
Var. OH *****	–	579	766	960
Fixed OH ******	–	342	397	447
Total C.O.S.	–	2278	2957	3655
Gross Profit	N.A.	544	774	1019

Note:

*	Same as Note 2 Danvers
**	Same as Note 3 Danvers
***	Ratio $3.033 ÷ $4.266 (Gainesville Labor – Danvers Labor) = 72%
****	Same as Note 3 Danvers
*****	Ratio $370,300 ÷ $457,083 (Gainesville Var. OH ÷ Danvers Var. OH) = 81% – See P & B Study
******	Ratio $248,642 ÷ $566,830 (Gainesville Fixed OH ÷ Danvers Fixed OH) = 44% – See P & B Study

Move Wood Operations to Gainesville

We will examine and comment on each segment of the P & B presentation:

LABOR

Danvers   The largest class of direct labor personnel at Danvers

falls into the Machine Operator B category. The 1976

labor rate for this task level is $3.52 per hour. (6% higher

than the 1975 level.) P & B's records indicate that the

factory efficiency at this location is 82.52% (1975). Thus:

$$\frac{\$3.52}{82.52\%} = \frac{\$4.266}{100\%}$$

Gainesville   The job classification at this plant, which is equal to that at

Danvers, is Grade 1 Assembler. The labor rate for this job

is $2.88 per hour. This is a day work classification.

Experience has shown the day work efficiency level here is

93.43%, thus:

$$\frac{\$2.88}{93.43\%} = \frac{\$3.083}{100\%}$$

The savings per labor hour are:

$$\begin{array}{r} \$4.266 \\ -\ 3.083 \\ \hline \$1,183 \end{array}$$

The 1976 budgeted labor hours for Wood are 106,534

106,534 x 1.183 = $126,030 savings

P & B has taken a conservative approach in the reported labor savings by using the

day work rate. After a training period (2 to 9 weeks), the jobs transferred to

82

Gainesville from Wood will become incentive based. The present incentive earnings at Gainesville average 125% (our observations indicated this level was easily achieved).

If an incentive level was chosen for a comparison with the Wood labor cost, we would obtain an even greater labor savings. Grade 1 Assembler, on incentive, earns $2.87 per hour. If we factor this rate by the incentive pace, we have an effective $2.30/hour labor cost at Gainesville!

Labor Variances

At Wood, labor variances have been running at 18.3% of the direct labor cost. At Gainesville, this figure runs to 6%. For our analysis, found in Exhibit B, we used the 18.3% Wood figure, assuming the variance is caused by the product, not the labor force.

Variable Overhead

Danvers

Actual variable overhead for this facility through 10/26/75, was 162.5% of direct labor cost.

Gainesville

The present variable overhead rate in this location is 159.4% for the same 10 month period as described above. This rate, however, is dependent upon Gainesville products. We have used the Wood rate of 162.5% and have factored it by the indicated savings.

Example: From the P & B Presentation

Danvers 1976 V.O.H.   – $457

Gainesville 1976 V.O.H.   – $370

370 – 457 = 81%

Thus, for each year the Gainesville variable overhead costs are 81% of the
comparible Wood V.O.H.

Contributing to the variable overhead savings at Gainesville is a reduction
(from Danvers levels) to 6 factory indirects. These include 4 assistant foremen,
1 personnel clerk and 1 cost accountant. All are functions which can be absorbed
by the present Gainesville labor force. Other variable savings are realized in
obviously non duplicated areas as office supplies, reproduction, stockroom supplies
and more.

Fixed Overhead

Danvers

As was the case in Variable, we obtained actual 1975 (thru 10/26/75)

fixed rate. It is 206.7% of D. L. hours. We used this

actual 206.7% in Exhibit A (1975).   To account for higher volumes in

subsequent years, the fixed overhead rates were not held constant, but

were increased by 1/2 the difference in rate for the present

and next year (See Exhibit B). We felt this procedure would yield a more

accurate position on fixed costs.

In using the 1975 Danvers' actual overheads for 1976 thru 1978, we may

have presented higher costs than may be experienced. However, the

differential in cost as outlined by P & B is the main objective. Since we used the same parameters for both Danvers and Gainesville, we are confident these differentials are accurate.

The reduction in fixed overhead is due to many things, some of which are:

o   Reduction of 2 exempt employees, 1 Operations Manager and
     1 Buyer

o   Reduction in lease and other attendent costs at Danvers

     Danvers lease – $40,200/year*

     Taxes $33,000/year

     Insurance $ 4,000
                    $77,200

* P & B has been very conservative in estimating a $40,200 return on a $70,200 lease at Danvers. (The $30,000 difference is added into the Fixed Overhead at Gainesville).

o   Reduction in building maintenance costs

o   Medical services, etc.

Relocation Costs

P & B has indicated a cost of $136,000 for affecting the move to Gainesville. We have no argument with any of the listed move costs, in fact, we have found them to be very well supported. We would, however, add to this $136,000 figure, the following:

1.   Cost of carrying inventory buffer ($42,000)   – $13,500
     ($142,000 max x .25 carrying charges) x .38 (20 wks.)

2.   Overtime premium to develop inventory   – $ 1,700
          $2,822,000 ÷ 106,534/hrs. – $26.49/hr.
          $142,000 ÷ 26.49 – 5,361/hrs
            5,361/hrs x $.31 (10% DL) = $1,662

3.   Labor inefficiency at Wood during phase out (est.) $ 10,000

4.   Contingency $ 18,000

We recommend the total implementation costs be increased to $180,000.

Training new operators and the attendant inefficiencies in direct labor and scrap

losses caused by such a relocation plan are considered by P & B. Rather than

breaking these costs out as a part of the relocation cost, they have chosen to add

them ($6,000 in training inefficiencies and $12,000 in rework) to the adjusted

Wood, at Gainesville, Variable Cost.

We feel both allocations are sufficient to cover these critical points.

   Example:

      55 direct labor operators x 40 hrs. x $3.08/hr = $6,776

      P & B has accounted for no production whatsoever for almost 1 full week

      (35 hrs.) for the total 55 workers required.

We had much discussion with P & B personnel concerning Severance Pay. The Danvers'

(Wood) contract does not have a severance pay clause. P & B had considered 4

seperate severance plans.

1.   Using the P & B Princeton Indiana contract, severance pay would total $64,627.

2.   Using AMF Policy 3-17, severance pay totaled $59,909.

3.   Assume a negotiated severance of 2 days pay for each year of service – $54,314

4.   Assume a negotiated severance of 1 week pay for every year thereafter – $48,429

P & B chose the highest of the listed plans. We feel the plan and cost chosen is

realistic.

Facilities Comparison

    Danvers

        Office = 4480 sq. ft.

        MFG   = 21,000 (includes storerooms, ship &receive & test)
              25,480 sq. ft.

Note: The Danvers' facility also includes space for:

          Engr. & Model Shop   1400 sq. ft.
          Rest Rooms   1240 sq. ft.
          Lunch rooms   1400 sq. ft.
                                  4040 sq. ft.

(Gainesville has space to accomodate these functions

    without duplication. The facility had supported a work force of

    588 in July 1974. (Present manning is under 400.)

    Gainesville

        Office =   860 sq. ft.

        MFG   = 9,000 sq. ft.
              9,860 sq. ft.

*Requires removal of present conference room.

The manufacturing space at Gainesville, although slightly smaller, is sufficient

to absorb the Wood, Danvers' Product Line. Additional manufacturing space at

Gainesville could be gained for subassembly work by using 1840 square feet of space

in the Heat Treat area. All or part of this area could be used since the workload in

this area is only 2 to 4 hours a week.

Our concern and one expressed by P & B also, is one of office space. The space

available at Gainesville is not sufficient to conduct an efficient operation. There

are alternative solutions to the problem, however. One would be to lease office space

nearby for non-manufacturing/engineering personnel, thus freeing space for those

whose function requires a "hands on" presence. Functions displaced could be
accounting, industrial relations, etc. A second would be to utilize a portion of
the present 2500 square feet canteen. A third, involving capital expenditures,
would be to build a 3,000 square foot addition in the open court   adjoining the
machine shop.

We recommend the first alternative. Implementing it would relieve the immediate
need for space and suffice to support the Gainesville operation until more permanent
solutions are found.

Should business conditions improve significantly as forecast by both Wood and
Gainesville, this Georgia plant will not be able to support it. However, since
Gainesville is now a plant whose products are "overflow" from other P & B locations,
It will be relatively simple to move these "overflow" items back to their original
manufacturing plants.

Freight In/Freight Out

Freight In

Due to the very nature of the Wood product, there will be very little
inbound or outbound freist costs should the Wood operation be relocated to Gainesville.
Almost 15% of the purchased parts new received in Danvers are produced in Gainesville
and shipped via P & B trucks. The extra freight costs incurred by the "unique" parts
will be offset by the savings in present Gainesville to Danvers Freight costs. Other
purchased items, with the exception of some molded parts for which older vendor
tooling is incompatible with present Georgia vendors, can be obtained locally.

Freight Out

At present, 60% of the Wood products are sold directly to OEM accounts, the bulk of these in the West. The remaining 40% are _now_ being distributed through P & B to jobbers. Since the total freight bill for outbound shipments is estimated to be less than 1/2 of 1% of total revenue in 1976, we have determined that any change in location will have a negligible effect on this small cost.

III.   PROBLEM SOLVING REPORTS

13.   A Lumber Company [A Bank Analyst's Report]

(Anonymous)

THE COMPANY: This report was provided by a regional
bank with over $3 million in total assets.
The bank is headquartered in a major metropolitan center in an Atlantic Coast
state and operates over 150 branch locations.

THE REPORT: The following report is an analyst's evaluation of an application for a major loan
from one of the bank's customers, "A Lumber Company," which wished to invest in a
kraft pulp mill. The report is indicative
of the broad research a report writer often
must pursue. In this case the analyst not
only had to know the banking business but
also had to know (or learn about) the lumber business. (The names of the companies
involved were changed at the contributing
bank's request. The symbol "M" in the report stands for thousands.)

May 24, 1977

MEMO TO:

FROM:

SUBJECT: A Lumber Company

   We have received audited financial statements for the fiscal year ended
November 30, 1976 from J. W. Doe & Co., CPAs,the usual accountants, who
expressed an unqualified opinion. These statements have been reviewed in
terms of our line commitment and term loan to this customer and in terms of
its planned investment in a proposed kraft pulp mill, Kraft Pulp, Inc.,
near a city in a Southeastern state.

Relationship

	1973	1974	1975	1976
Average Loan	$1,227.0M	$2,066.9M	$2,629.0M	$3,774.7M
Net Free Balances	404.5M	398.2M	215.8M	387.3M
Bal./Avg. Loan	33.0%	19.3%	8.2%	10.3%

   A $1,000.0M seasonal line has been made available to A Lumber Company
which expired February 28, 1977, and under which it has borrowed $1,400.0M,
being over its line since January of this year. The bank is also extending
$1,600.0M under a term loan agreement and $1,562.1M through the International
Division under Letters of Credit, bringing their total debt to $4,563.1M
presently. For the first five months of the company's fiscal year, it has
maintained net free balances averaging $201.6M, which is down from the
$387.3M averaged in 1976.

Industry Outlook

   For obvious reasons, the lumber industry is most closely tied to the
construction industry. As a result, the industry experienced its best year
ever in 1973 and its worst year since the Depression in 1975. Sales look
good into 1978, maybe as good as 1973, but profits may begin to slow by the
end of 1977 as labor and stumpage costs increase. Stumpage costs have
doubled since 1973.

   When housing starts exceed 1,500.0M per year, suppliers must begin to
order heavily from the Pacific-Northwest mills, which cut from public
lands at higher costs, driving prices up. Housing starts for 1977 are projected at 1,800.0M and since the West Coast is experiencing such dry weather,
the forests there may be closed in May rather than August or September because
of fire weather. This would certainly benefit East Coast suppliers. Further,
it is projected that as many as 1,200.0M of this year's housing starts may be
single family units, which use nearly twice as much lumber and plywood as
multiple family units.

91

During 1976, the South supplied only 8 billion board feet of the soft-
wood production and 4 billion board feet of the hardwood production out of
a total production of about 30 billion board feet. With half of the nation's
hardwood growing stock in the South, some estimate that the South may be
producing half of the nation's total lumber production by the year 2000.
This, coupled with the South's upward population trend providing labor and
requiring housing, places a strong Southern lumber producer in a very good
position for the future.

Forest Industries magazine publishes a comparison of major U. S. lumber producers each year during the summer. A Lumber Company is one of the top producers presented each year. It would be beneficial to obtain a copy of this publication when it becomes available.

Operations
(Dollars in Thousands)

(% of Net Sales)	1973	1974	1975	1976
Net Sales $	$21,096.4	$24,750.0	$25,890.3	$34,611.7
Gross Profit				
Margin %	35.5%	20.2%	12.1%	14.8%
SGA Expenses %	10.3	10.4	10.7	10.1
Interest Expense %	4.2	5.2	6.4	6.5
PBT %	22.3	5.3	(4.6)	(0.8)
Net Profit $	$2,367.2	$ 965.2	$(.615.5)	$ 93.2

On a 33.7% increase in sales to $34,611.7M, the company was able to show
a profit of $92.3M only by taking a $361.1M income tax refund. The gross
profit margin improved slightly, but not enough to return to the level of
profits experienced prior to 1974. Selling, General & Administrative expenses
continue to run about 10% of net sales. While these expenses seem well controlled, an analysis is not possible, since only a total expense is given for
this category.

A break down of Cost of Goods Sold is not provided either, so no statement can be made about the slight improvement made. Judging from previous profitable years, it would appear that the company needs to control the pricing
of products, or the cost of goods sold, to provide a gross profit margin of
25-30%, and to continue to maintain selling, general and administrative expenses
at current levels to generate the profits necessary to pay interest and meet
long-term debt curtails. Unfortunately, industry forcasts indicate that this
may not be possible as profit margins will continue to be squeezed by increased
labor and stumpage costs.

It should be noted that the substantial increase in total debt has caused
interest expenses to increase accordingly with a corresponding drain on profits.

A Dun & Bradstreet report dated January 14, 1977 shows trade payments being
made on a "prompt - slow 30 days" basis. This compares unfavorably with reports
for the two previous years, which show trade payments made on a "discount-prompt"
basis. This is an indication of cash flow pressures.

Balance Sheet
(Dollars in Thousands)

(% of Total Assets)	1973	1974	1975	1976
Total Assets $	$20,674.3	$25,679.8	$28,578.4	$37,006.3
Cash & A/R %	13.5	8.8	9.9	9.8
Inventory %	8.7	17.3	17.1	17.5
Timber, Land & Rights %	53.3	46.7	48.1	46.9
Plant, Prop. & Equip. %	19.6	19.4	17.6	19.3
Current Payables %	15.6	6.4	3.9	4.1
Current Maturities %	6.5	13.1	11.4	15.7
Net Long-Term Debt %	51.8	55.9	64.9	64.2
Total Debt %	73.9	75.4	80.3	84.7
Tang. Net Worth $	$5,395.1	$6,036.8	$5,397.4	$5,470.5
Ratios:				
Current	1.48	1.80	2.16	1.80
Quick	0.64	0.47	0.67	0.49
Debt/Worth	2.83	3.21	4.25	5.73

An analysis of the balance sheet as broken down above indicates several significant trends. A most important trend is seen in the growth of the level of debt. Current maturities of long-term debt have increased from 6.5% of total assets in 1973 to 15.7% of total assets in 1976. Long-term debt has increased similarly, growing from 51.8% of total assets in 1973 to 64.2% of total assets in 1976. The combination of these two increases and poor operating performance is reflected in the deteriorating debt/worth ratio from 2.83 in 1973 to 5.73 in 1976.

While total assets have increased by 79.0% since 1973, there has been no major shift in the asset mix as a percentage of total assets, except for the increase in inventory between 1973 and 1974 at the expense of cash and receivables. There have been some fluctuations in the value of timber, timberrights, and timber and farm lands, which seem to correspond to the company's use of its own timber resources. (The value of company timber used can be seen in the Funds Flow, chart below)

Because the company shows a portion of its own timber and timber rights which it expects to use during the current fiscal year as a current asset, its current ratio seems fairly adequate. However, this is somewhat deceptive since it will only become a current asset as long as market demand holds up and that timber is cut and converted to inventory. For this company the current ratio should delete the value of that expected timber usage. This would indicate current ratios of 1.03 for 1973, 1.36 for 1974, 1.78 for 1975 and 1.34 for 1976, which are not as favorable, and which, when compared to the quick ratio should cause creditors some concern. In a liquidation, lumber inventories could be subject to deterioration if not promptly moved.

In a note to the financial statements, the auditors indicate the company's major capital assets are significantly under valued at cost. They indicate that company land, shown at an average cost of $44.78 per acre, has a market value of $201.30 per acre for an appreciation of $19,1815M. The value of timber and rights is shown at $36.19 per Mean Board Foot (MBF) and should be shown at $55.00 per MBF for an appreciation of $5,898.8M It was also pointed out that the replacement value of the company's plants was nearly three times

their book value, and that fire insurance was carried at close to
replacement value. A proforma balance sheet showing these appreciations
indicates a $37,856.0M increase in net worth to $43,415.7M, giving considerably more coverage to creditors than the balance sheet shown at cost
or book value.

Funds Flow
(Dollars in Thousands)

	1973	1974	1975	1976	'73-'76 Average
Net Income (Loss)	2,367.2	965.2	(615.5)	92.3	702.3
Depreciation	625.6	905.3	1,137.7	1,296.9	991.4
Cost of Company Timber	2,227.5	2,349.2	1,911.2	4,019.5	2,626.9
Long Term Debt	1,864.2	5,186.8	6,481.1	6,604.9	5,034.3
Miscellaneous	125.9	(8.0)	(3.0)	200.8	78.9
Total Funds Provided	7,210.4	9,398.5	8,911.5	12,214.4	9,433.7
Purchase Timber & Rights	2,912.9	2,602.0	3,648.2	4,830.8	3,498.5
Purchase Real Estate	248.2	470.0	541.1	1,012.4	567.9
P/P/E	1,589.3	1,586.1	1,200.2	3,595.4	1,992.8
Current Long-Term Debt	1,902.1	1,541.5	2,284.0	1,412.6	1,785.0
Pfd. Stock Dividend	27.9	30.3	39.9	30.2	32.1
Miscellaneous	58.7	678.2	185.9	380.9	325.9
Total Funds Applied	6,739.1	6,908.1	7,899.3	11,262.3	8,202.2
Increase Working Capital	471.3	2,490.4	1,012.3	952.1	1,231.5
Cash Flow Coverage Ratio	1.81	1.72	0.74	1.30	

From the chart above, it can be seen that in spite of an accelerated depreciation
schedule, the company has been funding an average of only 49.7% of new P/P/E acqui-
sitions with non-cash charges. The cost of company timber has funded only 64.6%
of the past four years' of timber, timber land, and timber rights purchased and
capitalized. The balance of those capital aquisitions plus an average of 72.9%
of the current maturities of long-term debt have been funded primarily (87.8%) by
additional long-term debt and only secondarily (12.2%) by profits. Additional
long-term debt cannot continue to fund such a major portion of this company's
growth.

The cash flow coverage ratio shown above was computed using the following
formula:

$$\text{Cash Flow Coverage} = \frac{PBT + \text{Interest} = \text{Leases} + \text{Depreciation} + \text{Company Timber} + \text{Pfd. Dividend}}{\text{Interest} + \text{Leases} + \frac{\text{Principal Payments} + \text{Pfd. Dividends}}{1 - \text{Tax Rate}}}$$

A deteriorating cash flow coverage trend can be seen between 1973 and 1975.
The trend seems to reverse in 1976, but this was accomplished by doubling the amount
of company timber used over the previous year. Solving the equation to show a cash
flow of 1.00 for 1977 using the average figures for all elements except principal
payments, which are this year's actual maturities as of November 30, 1976,
and using a tax rate of 35%, the company must generate a Profit Before Taxes
of $5,362.7M. Given the slow first quarter reported by the company, indicating
a loss of $600.0M before taxes, it seems unlikely that the company can have a
positive cash flow without another refinance of current maturities and another
substantial increase in the use of its own timber. An alternative might be
for the company to sell some of its least valuable timber and timber rights
and/or to close and sell any unprofitable mills it may have.

Conclusions

    Admittedly, the averages used to project an appropriate profit level
for 1977 contain a number of impurities, but they are accurate enough to
indicate that the company will need to monitor its operations and utilize its
assets to their fullest extent to maintain its present condition. The
company will find it difficult enough to maintain present operations without
considering a posture of further expansion.

    In consideration of the fact that the company is approaching default
on the total debt and the worth/debt terms of our loan agreement as amended
on January 14, 1977, it seems apparent that modifications in the loan
agreement are again imminent. The cash flow problems of the company are
evident in its failure to meet the balance requirements of our loan agreements. The company does not have the cash available to proceed with the
Kraft Pulp project and proposed, among other means, to fund its contribution of $3,300.OM in part with seasonal lines of credit, which is not
a proper source of funds for a long-term capital investment.

    It would appear that it would be in the bank's best interest to hold
A Lumber Company to a commitment to consolidate its position further
before agreeing to any further expansion. While the lumber industry appears
strong in the long run, it may be subject to some financial pressures in the
short run. Because A Lumber Company has just gone through a major
expansion phase, it is in a position to benefit greatly from the expected
upturn in the industry, but it may suffer severely if allowed to commit to
any further expansion funded by debt. If the economy does not remain strong
enough to provide substantial profits, the company may be forced to deplete its
own timber resources to provide the cash needed for the debt service. Rapid
depletion of timber resources will be felt in an increase in the cost of goods
sold in subsequent years, adding more pressure to profits by decreasing profit
margins and by increasing the need to replace depleted timber resources.

    With regard specifically to the Kraft Pulp project, the file does
not contain sufficient information to evaluate it. The benefit to A
Lumber Company appears to be as a source of additional income through the
sale of a mill by-product. There is no indication whether this income will
provide an appropriate offset for the company's capital expenditure to gain
"chips" to other kraft processors, it may be better to continue this until the
company is in a better capital position to fund the project.

    With continued strong, active management, this company is positioned to
benefit by an upturn in the lumber industry, and to benefit to an even
greater extent by the growth expected in the Southeast. There are, however,
too many indications that the cash flow pressures on its highly leveraged
position could cause a serious financial crisis. It is this analyst's opinion
that the bank should exercise its control in this situation by advising the
company to restructure its debt and its operations to be in a position to handle
its cash flows from operations, rather than from increases in long-term debt,
before any further expansion is contemplated.

    /jms

IV.   PROPOSALS FOR EXPENDITURES

        Modern businesses are increasingly dependent on
electronic and mechanical hardware to manufacture and
market their products and services. Because of the
high cost of this hardware, decisions about when to
purchase and what to purchase are among the most difficult and important decisions a manager must make;
consequently, proposals to purchase equipment must be
well justified and written. The information they contain must be clear and persuasively presented.

        The following proposals for equipment purchases
were written by individuals in companies that vary
greatly in size and nature. Those differences and
the nature of their requests dictated the slightly
different strategies you will notice in these reports.

IV. PROPOSALS FOR EXPENDITURES

14. Replacement of Data Processing Computer System

(Carolina Casualty Insurance Company)

THE COMPANY: Carolina Casualty Insurance Company, located in Jacksonville, Florida, writes insurance only for commercial automobiles
and long haul trucks. Its premium volume
is $35,000,000. Carolina Casualty employs
94 people. James C. Blanton is President
of the company and Jack C. Lotz is Vice
President in charge of Accounting, Data
Processing and Investments.

THE REPORT: This report recommends and justifies the
purchase of a new computer system for Caro-
lina Casualty's Data Processing department.
Notice that before he presents any data on
the recommended new system, this writer ex-
plains why the company's old system needs
replacing. This approach not only helps
justify the request but also places emphasis on events that have taken place
since the previous memo on the computer
situation was written six months earlier.

June 7, 1977

TO: James C. Blanton

FROM: Jack C. Lotz

SUBJECT: Replacement of Data Processing
                Computer System

As reported to you in my memo of December 9, 1976, our present IBM Computer System 1401 is now obsolescent; this model having been first introduced in 1960.

In the last six months, the situation has changed as follows:

1. The equipment is breaking down more frequently, causing more lost time while IBM responds to the repair calls.

2. On April 27, IBM notified us that this equipment would no longer be maintained on service contracts after April 30, 1981. Maintenance after that date would only be available "on a time and material basis dependent upon the availability of skills and other resources such as parts, tools and test equipment".

3. On August 1, 1977, the Raytheon Corp., which maintains our four Potter Model 7295 Magnetic Tape Drives is increasing the monthly maintenance charge from $432 to $467 monthly. In addition, there is a possibility this maintenance engineer may be moved to Atlanta which would greatly increase the time it would take him to respond to a service call.

In view of the above, I recommend that we replace our present computer system. I further recommend that we do this by purchase of an IBM System 370 Model 115 Computer System for installation about July, 1978.

This system is a current model and has a greatly increased capacity which could be adapted to meet all conceivable growth needs over the next ten years. The purchase price from IBM would be $250,000 (less $25,000 investment tax credit for a net of $225,000).

Such data processing equipment is an admitted asset so there would be no effect on surplus on the purchase date. The cost to the company would show as a monthly depreciation expense of $2,083 over ten years.

A cost comparison with our present system is shown below:

	IBM 1401	IBM 370 Mod. 115
Depreciation	$ 476	$ 2,083
Maintenance	1,069*	1,095
	1,545	3,178

        *Eff. 8/1/77

At the end of April, the undepreciated value of our present IBM 1401 System was

Form 25

$14,286. There should be sufficient sales value to avoid any loss on this equipment, but there is also little chance of significant profit.

The IBM 370 Model 115 purchase price shown above is that quoted by the IBM Corporation for 9-month delivery. It is sometimes possible to obtain this model through used computer brokers at a substantial savings (15%-30%). This is the way we purchased our present IBM 1401 five years ago. I have contacted the American Used Computer Corporation and they will inform me if a computer meeting our requirements comes on the market. Such computers are eligible for direct maintenance from the IBM Corporation and may be purchased subject to inspection.

Finally, I want to present some additional details on this recommendation:

1. Purchase vs. lease. The monthly lease of the proposed machine is $7,191. Comparing this to the purchase cost plus monthly maintenance shows that after two and one-half years, it becomes cheaper for the company to purchase rather than lease. We anticipate a usage period of 10 years.

2. IBM vs. another manufacturer. IBM has the most comprehensive engineering and systems support locally. In addition other major companies have withdrawn from the computer field such as Xerox, leaving their customers with decreasing support. We have this problem with our present tape drives, made by the Potter Company.

3. IBM Mod. 370 vs. IBM System 3. IBM now has two computer divisions that compete with each other. The General Products Division has the System 3, which is used, for example, by Gulf American Insurance Company in Montgomery, Alabama. The Data Processing Division has the System 370 which is used, for example, by Canal Insurance Company.

The System 370 is a more powerful computer than the System 3 and is more expensive. The real value of the System 370 is that it will operate under our existing programs, of which we have some 250 active, developed over the last 17 years. To rewrite all of these programs before we could use a System 3 would be a mammoth task, requiring additional programmers. It is true that the programs will eventually be rewritten to take advantage of the new machines. However, we have found in the past, as in the recent change from a punched card system to a magnetic tape system, that the change is smoother for all departments of the company, and can be done with existing employees, when it is accomplished gradually over a period of time rather than as a one time complete system change.

JCL:bf

IV. PROPOSALS FOR EXPENDITURES

15. Proposal for Purchase of Video Tape Equipment

(Saunders Leasing System, Inc.)

THE COMPANY: Saunders Leasing System, Inc. is in the full service long term vehicle leasing business (trucks, trailors, and tractors). It employs approximately 1600 people in its headquarters in Birmingham, Alabama, and in its offices and service centers across the country.

THE REPORT: This report recommends the purchase of color video tape equipment to support Saunders's extensive training programs for sales, administrative, and service personnel.

COMPANY CORRESPONDENCE

January 20, 1977

TO: Don Stevenson

FROM: Brown Saunders

SUBJECT: Proposal for Purchase of Video Tape Equipment

I am proposing that we purchase Video Tape Recording and Replay equipment for use in training this year.

Initial Purchase for Use in 1977

The initial purchase proposed would give us the capability to record and play back (a) training presentations, (b) briefing meetings, (c) role play sessions (sales training) and (d) practice lectures such as those planned for the Instructor Training Program.

The initial purchase proposed is portable and will allow us to record new or improved techniques and methods at the local facilities for replay in training sessions, meetings and workshop/seminars.

As an added bonus, this equipment will allow us to record special programs for future use. For example, we could have recorded the 60th Anniversary Party.

Below is the estimated cost of the proposed initial purchase, both black and white (monochrome) and color, and based on quotes obtained in December, 1976.

Items Proposed for Purchase	Cost	
	Color	Black & White
Camera (incl. lens, tripod, headset, mic)	$ 5,900	$ 1,900
19" Receiver	580	240
Portable Recorder	3,000	2,000
Portable Lighting Kit	495	495
Associated Connector Panels, Cables, Cabinets	500	500
Total	$10,475	$ 5,135

January 20, 1977
Video Tape Equipment Proposal

Of the comparison above, I prefer to spend the additional money
and purchase color for the reasons stated below.

1. The color equipment proposed is standard and is compatible
with studio equipment that can be added as use and need demand.

2. Even though black and white would be adequate for role play
use, color has, by far, the more credibility with the audience.

3. Color also does a better job of definition, especially under
marginal light conditions, for black and white shows up simply
as various shades of gray. For example, red and green are easily
definable to the normal eye in color, but they record as almost
the same shade of gray in monochrome.

The equipment listed above can be put to meaningful use immediately
with only a minimum amount of operator training required. However,
this equipment will not give us the capability to produce finished
presentations, complete with titles, special effects, etc. We
will also be limited in the availability of commercially produced
programs because they are sold in 3/4" casettes as compared to the
1/2" casette used in the proposed portable recorder.

Future Plans and Possibilities

Before we can produce finished presentations for reproduction and
distribution to the Regions, we will need additional equipment
and additional training of our present staff.

The estimated cost of the additional equipment necessary to accomplish the editing and reproduction of finished programs and presentations is as follows:

Item	*Cost	
	Color	Black and White
Studio Record/Edit/Playback System	$13,390	$13,390
Receiver/Monitor/Demodulator	640	280
Additional Connector Panels Cables and Cabinets	495	495
Total Editing and Supportive Equipment	$14,525	$14,165

*Cost based on quotes received in late December, 1976.

January 20, 1977
Video Tape Equipment Proposal

Since the studio record/edit/playback equipment above is of 3/4"
format, we will be able to take advantage of commercially produced programs available for purchase. Training films, once
available only in 16 mm movie format, are now available in 3/4"
video tape cassettes, and one company, Advanced Systems, Inc.,
lists over 750 different video tape programs for rent or purchase
and new subjects are being added every month.

It is anticipated that when we begin producing finished presentations, we will need a remote playback unit in each Region.
Currently, the cost to each Region would be less than $1000 for
the playback unit plus the cost of a color television receiver.

Summary

I feel that Video Tape is the Audio Visual Training medium of the
future and that we should proceed to acquire the equipment described
in the Initial Purchase for Use in 1977. It's acquisition and use
will be of significant benefit to our in-house training programs this
year and in our total effort in the future.

HBS/jr

IV. PROPOSALS FOR EXPENDITURES

16.   Request Approval of a Capital Appropriation

(Anonymous)

THE COMPANY: The company which provided this report is
                  a large manufacturing company which pro-
                  duces and markets a wide variety of goods
                  through domestic and foreign divisions.

THE REPORT: This report is a request for the purchase
                  of a 350 kilowatt emergency generator to
                  protect a large manufacturing plant from
                  freeze damage caused by a long winter power
                  failure. Notice that the writer of this
                  report has already sought advice from per-
                  sonnel in several other divisions of his
                  company and draws upon their opinions to
                  support his recommendation in this report.
                  ("THE CORPORATION" and "Northern Plant"
                  are names I have added to clarify re-
                  ferences in the report.)

THE Corporation _____INTRA CORPORATION

Date: January 23, 1978

To:
Location: Controller

From: Manager
Location: Domestic Financial Planning and Analysis

Subject: Request Approval of a Capital Appropriation

Division: Northern Division - Northern Plant

Investment Requested: 350KW Generator $44,168

Proposed Method of Financing: Internal Funds

Purpose: To replace a 100KW generator with a 350KW generator
          for the emergency electrical system.

Project Description:

During the winter months, the Northern Plant is vulnerable to severe
damage from freezing should an interruption of electrical power occur.
It has been estimated that with an outside air temperature of 0°F, in
less than four hours the steam lines, color lines, fire protection
sprinkler lines and water supply lines would start to freeze, resulting
in considerable water damage from the bursting pipes.

To avoid the risk of such extensive damage, the Northern Plant is request-
ing a 350KW generator to replace the existing 100KW generator purchased
in 1975. In addition to being an emergency power source for sump pumps
and lighting, as was the 100KW generator, the requested unit will allow
the Northern Plant to run the oil fired package boiler. This will
permit the building to be heated to a plant protection level and insure
a resumption to full production when the electrical outage is corrected.

Project Analysis:

Northern Plant has stated they have not experienced a power loss which
lasted for over two hours in fifteen years. However, in 1976, an ice
storm in southern Wisconsin resulted in several areas being without
power for three weeks. Damage to the mill from an extended power outage
such as the one in southern Wisconsin, if it were to occur in Northern,
could cause extensive damage running into the millions of dollars.

Risk Management & Insurance and the Real Estate Division have reviewed
this project and recommend its approval. They point out that THE CORPORATION'S
business interruption and property damage insurance coverage is written
with an annual aggregate million dollar deductible. Typically, the
annual loss currently experienced under this coverage is $400,000.

Therefore, the incremental exposure to loss at the Northern Plant is
approximately $600,000. Risk Management & Insurance believes this
investment is prudent, considering the possibility of extensive damage
from a prolonged power outage. The existing 100KW generator will be traded
in at $5,000 over its original cost, against the purchase of this new 350KW
generator.

Recommendation:

Real Estate and Risk Management & Insurance agree that this investment
provides adequate protection of the plant and equipment against an
extended winter power outage at a reasonable cost. We therefore
recommend approval of this request.

DJE:SEF:mlc

Approved: _____
                                   Director, Financial Planning and Analysis

V. BUSINESS FORECASTS

Business managers are always trying to look into the future. They are interested in past events and present conditions mainly as indicators of what might be happening in the future that might affect their businesses. Without some sense of what might happen based on what has happened and is happening, the business manager is forced to make blind decisions about future operations; good forecasts can never take all the blindness out of those decisions about the future, but they can help the manager see clearly enough to make informed decisions in which he or she can be reasonably confident.

The forecasts included here take different forms. The first assesses a division's progress to date as a foundation for setting goals and objectives for the following year. The second is a brief, but detailed overview of the national economy for the next year with a special emphasis on how particular economic trends might affect a particular industry. The third is simply an analysis of current economic conditions in a particular city and state; the "forecast" is more implied than stated and is left mainly to the reader. In all these reports, however, the purpose is the same--to help the business manager guess with more confidence and accuracy about what the future might hold.

V. BUSINESS FORECASTS

17. Goals and Objectives for 1977/WHN

(Storer Broadcasting Company)

THE COMPANY: Storer Broadcasting Company owns and operates a number of radio and TV broadcasting
stations as well as community TV antenna
services. The company employs 1,773 people
at its headquarters in Miami Beach, Florida, and in its operating stations in other
locations.

THE REPORT: Periodically businesses must review their
progress and then look ahead and set realistic goals. In this report to his superiors at Storer Broadcasting, the manager
of WHN, a "country music" radio station
located in New York City, projects his
goals for the station's next year of operation based on its current position.
(The figures and percentages under "REVEN-
UES" have been deleted at the company's
request.)

50,000 WATTS
WHN
1050

STORER RADIO, INC.

400 PARK AVENUE,
NEW YORK 22
MURRAY HILL 8-1000

DATE   November 12, 1976

SUBJECT   Goals and Objective
for 1977/WHN

To   Mr. Terry H. Lee

From   Neil Rockoff

Background: We are in the midst of finalizing our submission
for WHN's "operating budget for the full year 1977". In
order to try and come closest to a realistic GROSS REVENUE
figure I have waited these few extra days in order to allow
for a better feel in regard to revenues.

As I understand it the "goals and objectives" memo, is to
deal with the general areas of the radio station and therefore expands upon the operating budget narrative in that it
delves into other areas of the station in sweeping import.

Here then for your information is the essence of my "goals
and objectives" for 1977 as they impact upon the operation
of WHN in general.

REVENUES

At this point it looks as though we'll be trying to
achieve a gross revenue output of some $ minimally
for 1977. This should generate a minimum "upper" bottom
line (OPERATING PROFIT BEFORE DEPRECIATION) of $
This should be (by year's end we'll know for sure)
approximately a three-fold increase over the "upper"
bottom line of 1976 and approximately an   % increase
in gross revenues over 1976 (which represented what will
be approximately a   % increase over 1975 gross
revenues.

RATINGS

Our rating goals for 1977 will parallel the new Arbitron
radio demographic sell data which will change the
perennial 25-49 demographic we have always sought to
a choice of 25-44 or 25-54. This is so as noted above
because Arbitron is now going from 35-49 and 50-64
demographic cells to 25-34 / 35-44 / 45-54 / 55-64 and
65 and over. The teens (12-17 and 18-24 data stays
the same. The objective for us therefore is to determine
wisely whether or not we go for the 25-44 or 25-54
demographics. Of course the right choice will be
tremendously beneficial to us whereas the wrong choice
(even if executed properly) could be very costly to us
in terms of agency billing. We therefore have determined
that because of the nature of country music and its
base of basically middle aged adult listenership that
we will primarily go after the 25-54 age bracket.
This will give us cause to fine-tune minute changes in
programming parameters to pick up this additional
five chronological years of audience that we haven't
sought in the past while we were generating 25-49
demographic strengths.

PROGRAMING

Along the lines of the new rating cell as noted above
(that is 25-54 rather than 25-49 as a new target) our
music will change ever so slightly in older direction
while our contesting and on-air promotion will continually
appeal to the 25-34 segment of the population.

In addition to our music/contesting/on-air promotion
efforts for 1977 (which will be accelerated) we also
are very much interested in pursuing unique public
affairs and news programing. Currently our "WHN: In
the Public Interest" and our newly implemented "WHN: The
Sunday Report" are both unique in New York radio in
terms of their format and time span covered weekly.
We would like to continue to innovate in these two
important areas of our license commitment.

PROGRAMING (continued):

In addition to the above, an important goal of this
manager is to investigate fully the manpower requirements and needs as well as budgetary commitments
needed to initiate editorialization in 1977. Not
only does the fact that we have become one of the New
York market's most popular radio stations, but also
the fact that "country music" generates an audience that
would, we feel, tremendously be interested in issues
that affect their particular locale as opposed to
issues that affect the national scene. Of course we
do have a "mass appeal" format but we, on the other
hand, do have many of the above-noted "country"
listeners.

PROMOTION:

WHN in the past year or so has developed one of the
most highly visible and widely praised promotional
campaigns ever in radio circles. The promotion of
course was based on a "marketing strategy" and therefore it was more than "just a pretty face". Nonetheless
it also was awarded the distinction among all broadcast
properties in America of being an Effie finalist and
nominee in the past several months. It's noteworthy
to mention again that the nomination represented the
only broadcast property so honored in America and it
was the only nominee in all categories of the judging
that was not represented by an agency.

Anyway, the promotion plans for 1977 include a flirtation
with a radical shift (but along the same philosophical
aims) in our external and on-air contesting approach.
The reasoning would be to hit a new plateau in mass
appeal audience growth. Dependent upon the outcome of
the October/November 1976 survey (which we should have
and have fully analyzed by mid-December of this year)
we will so consider or not consider the "dramatic on-air
and external promotion campaign" shift in emphasis.

113

RECONSTRUCTION

Our goal to have one of the very best technical AM
facilities in broadcasting at a fabulous location
(54th and Park Avenue) will hopefully become a reality
before the spring of 1977 comes to a close. This
installation will afford us a facility that is safe,
pleasant and efficient and should add greatly to the
worth of WHN. The merchandising of this "new dedication
and physical manifestation of WHN's 'class' and
'greatness'" will be promoted and highlighted to the
agency community as well as creating an awareness of
our "new radio station" to the business community in
general.

FM SISTER STATION

One of the primary objectives of 1977 is to have
negotiated, programmed and implemented a new FM station
in the middle of 1977 so as to synergistically create
a larger revenue and audience base than WHN plus one
other radio station would cummulatively deliver. The
synergism of the two (if properly programmed and
managed) could create as noted above, revenue and
operating profit before depreciation parameters that
will make the "WHN/W---" operation a very meaningful
contributor to Storer Broadcasting Inc.'s broadcast
division annual report.

IN GENERAL

Generally, my goal is to continue to motivate what I
feel is the best management team, pound for pound in the
business today. It has youth, major market experience,
longevity in radio, and constant success as a common
denominator and continuing trademark of its greatness.
My goal is to expand upon this concept which has
originally been based on the philosophy of "pay the
good salary" to fewer people who are better experienced,
more dedicated and more professional under the concept
that "good people" produce and excel far beyond their
numerical contribution and therefore should be rewarded
for that continuity of employment and loyalty to company
and goals.

Mr. Terry H. Lee   -5-   November 12, 1976

IN GENERAL (continued):

Generally, I would like to think that by this week next
year, management of WHN can be talking about an
eminently more prestigious combination of radio
stations that it controls in New York, an incredibly
more profitable one with a continuity in personnel
at the department head level that will allow for the
final phase development (that is 1978) which was part
and parcel of the original 1975 three year plan. By
properly executing the aforementioned objectives with
the present department head management team, the
general manager of WHN should have no problem in
achieving the 1978 objectives which a year from today
should catapult the WHN stations to a competitive
position for "return on investment" with some of
Storer's other broadcast properties.

I hope this helps.

/p

V. BUSINESS FORECASTS

18. The Economy and Steel Through 1980

     (Armco, Inc.)

THE COMPANY: Armco, Inc. is a steel producer with head-
                quarters in Middletown, Ohio. In addition
                to various steel products, the company man-
                ufactures oil and mine field equipment and
                non-ferrous composite materials and is in-
                volved in insurance and finance leasing.
                It employs 50,322 people.

THE REPORT: This report is the 1979 version of the eco-
                nomic outlook report prepared yearly by
                Armco's Chief Economist. The report gives
                an overview of the national economic pic-
                ture and then focuses specifically on the
                outlook for steel and other market segments
                in which Armco is involved.

116

commercial research bulletin

Paul C. Harmon
Chief Economist
December 7, 1979

THE ECONOMY AND STEEL THROUGH 1980

ECONOMIC OUTLOOK: ANOTHER SKIRMISH IN THE WAR ON INFLATION

The on-again off-again recession of 1979 which began in the
second quarter, and took a time-out in the third, is definitely
on again, and the key question now is, "How bad will it be
in 1980?" Out of the key question comes a host of others.
Will the Fed squeeze too hard or not hard enough? Will consumers
quit buying? Will housing collapse? How much will OPEC demand
for oil? Are inventories dangerous? Will there be another
run on the dollar? What about Iran? The list could go on
and on.

Most of these questions are so intertwined that the answer
to any one of them depends on the answers to several others.
Thus one is forced to sort through a nearly endless tangle
of possible combinations and come up with a scenario that
fits best with today's facts, and hope that random shocks,
especially the unfavorable variety, are minimal.

Looking at the big consumer sector first, not much has changed
in recent months. Buying power continues to erode under the
constant pounding of inflation, and this winter, growing unemployment will add to the problem. On the positive side,
however, things may not be quite as dreary as portrayed by
official government statistics. Incomes are higher and probably
growing faster than reported, and at the same time, the Consumer
Price Index overstates the negative impact of inflation on
many consumers.

Reasons for under-reported income are not hard to find, but
documentation of the amount is. With double-digit inflation
and increasing awareness of the tax-bracket ripoff, the
attractiveness of moonlighting, 'off-the-books' transactions,
cash deals and barter is rising, and such practices are spreading.
As for the CPI in a period of sharply rising prices, the impacts
are twofold. First, most consumers adjust the quantities
of different things they buy as prices change, but the Index
measures the price of a 'fixed basket' of items every month.
Secondly, zooming house prices and mortgage rates inflate
the index as computed monthly when in fact, only a small minority
of all consumers buy houses in any given month. This leads
to the kind of anomalous situation in which workers with cost

of living wage escalators and living in homes bought years
earlier at much lower prices and mortgage rates are compensated
in part as if they renegotiated their housing cost each month.

Those considerations aside, the outlook for consumer spending
remains precarious. Debt loads are heavy, and high interest
rates along with tightened lending practices will continue
to dampen 'buy-now-pay-later' psychology. Again, in the matter
of housing, the slowdown in sales accompanied by weakening
prices in some areas is reducing the flow of spendable cash
from inflated equity. Auto sales will be the major victim
of these developments. There are no signs, however, that consumers are losing their conviction that housing is the best
available inflation hedge. As a result, those now temporarily
sidelined by record mortgage rates and stiff down payments
will return to the market as soon as credit conditions permit.
There has been some restructuring of home financing to prevent
a complete drought of funds, but even with these innovations,
interest rates are still important.

Consequently, housing depends on Federal Reserve policy over
the next few quarters. Unless high interest rates and mortgage
unavailability collapse the market completely, including the
price structure, housing should be among the leaders of the
next upturn. An encouraging sign here is the recent downtick
in short term rates, largely because of weaker demand for
business loans. If indeed, this is the long-awaited peak
in interest rates or even a plateau, there are grounds for
belief that the Fed will not put the economy through a full-
fledged liquidity squeeze to blunt inflationary pressure.
So far, the Fed's moves have attracted no criticism, but that
will change as the economy slumps in the months ahead.

As mentioned on other occasions though, the Fed must now keep
one eye on the dollar in foreign exchange markets while trying
to keep the domestic economy on an even keel. The two needs
are not always compatible, practically assuring that some
hard choices will have to be made in an election year. And
just to complicate things, there is the chicken-and-egg sequence
in which rising oil prices are permitted to contribute to
U.S. inflation which weakens the dollar which in turn leads
to more pressure for higher oil prices by OPEC.

During 1979, oil prices were a semi-disaster. We believe
the odds for a repeat performance in 1980 are somewhat less.
Part of the 1979 surge in spot market prices which induced
higher OPEC prices came from a worldwide buildup in inventories
which is now beginning to strain storage capacity. Simultaneously
worldwide growth of consumption has slowed down in response
to price. In the U.S., the largest user, consumption is actually
declining fractionally. The recession will reduce demand in

the U.S. even more through all or most of 1980. By the second
half, the same may be true in other industrialized countries
as they slip into recession. On the surface, reduced demand
should help to stabilize prices, but that, of course, depends
on whether or not OPEC reduces output proportionately. Even
if they do, it is our judgment that oil prices will be less
troublesome in 1980, barring a complete blowup of the explosive
mixture of religion, oil and politics.

The first half of next year should also see an improving foreign
trade balance for the U.S. as import demand tails off due to
our recession while exports remain relatively strong. This,
along with tenuous prospects for more stability in oil prices
would contribute to dollar stability, if not strength, and
make the Fed's job a little easier. The major remaining fly
in the ointment will be a persistently high rate of inflation.

There are no real signs of slowdown in the rate of inflation
today, but conditions shaping up for the first quarter could
produce some. It appears now that recent monetary moves will
accelerate inventory liquidation. In many instances, after-
tax costs of carrying stock are now above any reasonable expectation of future price increases, making a good case for liquidation even if it means cutting prices. While this is only a
one-shot affair that does little to reduce underlying cost
inflation, it would be a welcome change from the endless string
of recent reports showing no progress at all.

In summary, developments which have taken shape in the two months
since the Fed summarily jacked up the cost of credit suggest
a somewhat earlier and deeper slide into the real recession
of 1980. Even under the old 'too-little-too-late' policy of
former Chairman Miller, recession was inevitable, but the
emergence of another run on the dollar and the threat of specu-
lative hyperinflation speeded things up. The first quarter
will get the brunt of inventory liquidation, production cutbacks
and layoffs. The second quarter will remain low, and second
half recovery will be anemic.

The recession will contribute little or nothing to the solution
of longer range structural problems of inflation, energy and
productivity. Congress and the Administration are not yet
ready to confront them, and most of the public is unaware of
their significance. That leaves the Federal Reserve, which
by itself, cannot solve them either. It can only continue to
try to moderate the economy's short term reactions to them,
and that means that current inflation restraint is but one
more move in a continuing zigzag search for painless solutions.

STEEL INDUSTRY: WEAK CONSUMPTION AND INVENTORIES
              CLOBBER FIRST HALF '80 SHIPMENTS

The steel industry will register its best year in 1979 since
1974. Shipments are almost certain to top 100 million tons.
Unfortunately, part of 1979's good showing represents business
borrowed from 1980. Given the signs of oncoming recession
in the second half of 1979, one might have expected steel
users to cut steel inventories. For several reasons that did
not happen. One is that outside of the auto industry, most
businesses saw few concrete signs in their orders or sales
that the much talked-about recession was going to affect them.
Others were simply unable to shut off the flow of incoming
steel from orders placed earlier in the year.

As a result, steel customers will start into 1980 with stocks
close to 3 months of supply even after an estimated reduction
of around 1 million tons in November and December. The combination of high interest rates since October and increasing
recessionary trends should spur efforts to get stocks down
in the final two months of 1979. Fortunately steel inventories
are at a much lower peak now that they were in 1975. Back
then, consumers had a 4½ month supply which took nearly two
years to bring back into line with a falling rate of usage.

For all of 1980, our market-by-market roundup indicates a
drop of 7.3 million tons in domestic steel consumption. In
the last recession, consumption dropped 14 million tons, and
in the one prior to that (1969-70), it fell 9.2 million.
However, as in all steel cycles, falling consumption is compounded by steel inventory liquidation, and the current cycle
will be no exception.

The combined impact of lower usage and inventory cutting will
have its most severe impact on industry shipments in the first
half of 1980. At our forecast volume of 43.5 million tons
in the first six months, shipments by the industry will be
10 million less than the same period in 1979. From midyear
on, the comparisons become less unfavorable as second half
1980 shipments of 46.7 million come within a million tons of
this year's closing half total. Comparing full year tonnages,
1979 is now estimated at 100.7 million and 1980 is forecast
at 90.2 million, a drop of 10.4 percent.

As always, forecasts of shipments by U.S. mills are subject
to the vagaries of foreign trade movements. For 1980, exports
have been put at 2.5 million tons, down a bit from 1979 on
the grounds that some of the other industrialized countries
will be entering recession as 1980 unfolds. More importantly,

foreign steel imports are estimated at 16 million tons in
1980 as compared with 17.1 million this year. The lower total
stems from the weak first half domestic market in conjunction
with trigger prices which prevent huge price reductions just
to move steel into the U.S. market.

The major downside risks to a 90 million ton shipment forecast
for 1980 are (1) a worse recession resulting in lower consumption
and (2) even heavier inventory cutting. On the upside, lower
imports raise U.S. mill shipments on a ton for ton basis.
This would partially offset the downside losses if the overall market tended toward greater weakness.

MAJOR MARKET OUTLOOK

Automotive Vehicle
and Parts Production
                                        -5.6% in 1979
                                        -10.5% in 1980

The temporary rebound in auto sales mentioned in our September
Bulletin has ended. Domestic auto sales in both October and
November, 1979, were off sharply from year ago levels. Our
sales forecast for 1979 is essentially unchanged at 10.6 million
total and 8.3 million domestic units. Auto production for
this year is expected to be 8.4 million units, a decline of
8.9% from 1978.

Continuation of inflation plus recent moves by the Federal
Reserve - which will further slow the economy and make auto
financing more difficult - have led to a downward revision
of 320 thousand units in our 1980 sales forecast. Total auto
sales for 1980 are now expected to equal 9.5 million units;
7.6 million of which will be domestic. Domestic auto production is similarly reduced to 7.6 million units in 1980, a
decline of 9.4% from 1979. U.S. truck production, which will
be off over 16% in 1979, is expected to decline an additional
13% in 1980 due to sluggish demand and uncomfortably high
inventory levels.

Construction Put-in-Place	-2.9% in 1979; -7.1% in 1980
Residential	-6.8% in 1979; -9.9% in 1980
Nonresidential	0 % in 1979; -5.0% in 1980

Until the Federal Reserve's October 6 decision to raise the
discount rate and pay more attention to monetary growth tar-
gets, housing activity seemed to be headed for a mild cycle.
The Fed's move to combat inflation by raising interest rates,
however, has substantially changed the 1980 housing forecast.
In the states with usury limits on mortgage rates, the availability of home financing has been restricted. In those states
without usury laws, the cost of mortgage loans has reached
record high levels thus pricing many potential homebuyers
out of the market.

Housing starts are expected to average 1.5 million units in
1980, down 13% from the 1.7 million starts projected this year.
Translated into actual construction work, residential construction put-in-place is forecast to decline 9.9% in 1980 after
falling 6.8% this year.

Commercial and industrial building sectors relate directly
to business activity but with a delayed response. Business
construction plans for 1980 are expected to be scaled down
as a result of falling plant utilization and housing activity
in 1979. The combined commercial and industrial construction
spending in constant dollars is forecast to decline 7.4% in
1980, ending a spending boom that saw 1979 inflation-adjusted
expenditures rise 11.2%.

In addition to depressed private construction, public construction spending is expected to decline in real terms in 1980.
Federal public works programs have been scaled down in the
budget as a sign of Congressional fiscal restraint. In total,
nonresidential construction put-in-place expressed in constant
dollars is predicted to fall 5% in 1980 after coming in
essentially flat this year.

| Service Centers: Composite Market Demand | +2.1% in 1979 |
| | -5.2% in 1980 |

Steel service centers have been selectively affected by the
current economic downturn. With strength from the capital
goods sector overshadowing weakness in the consumer durables
industries, demand for steel service center products is expected to increase 2.1% in 1979. However, as the economy
softens further, demand in 1980 is expected to decrease by

5.2%. Current inventory levels of industrial steel products
at service centers are reported to be within normal ranges
as compared to shipments. Implications are that the total
volume of steel shipments from U.S. mills to service centers
plus their import purchases will be up in 1979 and then decline
in 1980.

Machinery
          Nonelectrical   +5.9% in 1979; -6.6% in 1980
          Electrical Equipment +7.9% in 1979; -8.6% in 1980

Both machinery sectors are registering healthy production
gains for the fourth consecutive year. However constant
dollar orders for total machinery and manufacturers capacity
utilization, two leading indicators of machinery production,
both began evidencing weakness during the third quarter of
this year. Machinery production itself should soften through
the middle of 1980, after which signs of recovery are expected
to appear. Slowing in this sector reflects the next year's
outlook for a 6.7% decline in investment in producers durable
equipment, over 50% of which is typically made in machinery.

Oil and Gas Drilling   +3.7% in 1979
                                       +5.4% in 1980

Domestic drilling is recovering nicely from the first half
slump of 1979. Rotary rigs making hole in mid-November reached
the highest level in more than 20 years with oil drilling
leading the pace of the recovery.

Our 1979 footage forecast remains at 240 million feet, but
we have revised our 1979 forecast of well completions from
49,214 to 50,146 to reflect the greater concentration on oil
drilling. Our 1980 forecast of footage drilled has been
increased from 251 million feet to 253 million feet with
well completions raised from 52,325 to 53,085. Greater concentration on oil drilling will lower average well depth
a bit from 4,786 feet in 1979 to 4,767 feet in 1980. The
active rig count is expected to average 2,426 in 1980, up
12% from the 1979 level of 2,166.

Steel Weighted
Appliance Composite   -6.8% in 1979
                                       -6.3% in 1980

Healthy gains in retail sales of household appliances during
most of 1979 have curbed some of the softening originally
anticipated in that market. Production activity remains
weak in the heavy appliance sector however and most likely
will continue to be sluggish for most of 1980. Manufacturers'
inventories of appliances have been reduced considerably
this year, but indications are that further liquidation due
in part to higher carrying costs is a likely occurrence.
Declining housing completions during 1980 are also expected
to contribute to lower appliance production for next year.

Other Domestic and
Commercial Equipment   +2.8% in 1979
                                       -1.5% in 1980

Declining growth in personal consumption expenditures for
durables is evident in weakening ODCE production. This market,
which includes such products as furniture, technical instruments
and sporting goods, will probably continue to soften for
the first half of 1980 as overextended consumers take a type
of forced break from the recent year's spending spree. ODCE
production has been growing steadily since 1976, with an annual
expansion rate of close to 6% being the norm from 1977 until
first half of 1979. The expected slowdown next year should
still leave production above 1973's prerecessionary levels.

Railroad Equipment   +33.0% in 1979
                                       +6.0% in 1980

A combination of continuing demand for railroad cars and
increased component and carbuilding capacity has kept 1979
production in this market at record levels. Despite one
major cancellation, the order backlog for freight cars amounts
to about 18 months' production. This factor coupled with
a 6% increase in new orders of freight cars for the first
nine months of '79 over the same period 1978, implies that
strong production in the railroad equipment market will again
prevail in 1980.

Rails and Trackwork   +17.3% in 1979
                                        +4.0% in 1980

Several sustaining factors have influenced the ambitious rail
and trackwork buying spree contributing to lofty expected
shipment gains in 1979. Some of these factors are the deferred
track maintenance that remains to be overcome, increased
constant dollar operating revenues, the addition of rail
producing capacity, and growing traffic loads due to a modal
shift from truck to rail service. These factors are expected
to have a restraining effect on railroad management to run
for cover during the business downturn in 1980.

Farm Equipment Production   +9.2% in 1979
                                        -2.5% in 1980

Agricultural equipment production is expected to grow 9.2%
this year but decline in 1980. Retail farm equipment sales,
while strong in the first quarter, declined in second and
third quarter 1979 versus one year ago and are not expected
to rebound next year. Although manufacturers are expected
to add to inventories next year, total equipment production
should drop 2.5% in 1980.

Shipbuilding   -2.0% in 1979
                                        -3.6% in 1980

Strong demand for fishing vessels, barges to haul grain and
coal, oil drilling rigs, and repair and conversion work will
not offset the negative factors in this market. Dwindling
order backlogs and new orders for smaller merchant vessels
combined with an indecisive naval shipbuilding plan, contribute
to a pessimistic outlook for the U.S. shipbuilding industry
for 1979 and 1980.

Mining, Quarrying, & Lumbering   +7.2% in 1979
                                         0 % in 1980

Despite a bleak year for the coal industry, production has
soared above last year's strike-ridden level. Some inventory
building is expected to occur in the last half of 1980 in
anticipation of a strike in 1981. Lumber production is expected to be down in '79 and '80 along with residential construction. Metal mining and stone mining should post moderate
growth in 1979 and decline in 1980.

Aircraft and Parts   +17.4% in 1979
                                         +6.4% in 1980

In September, the Federal Reserve Board's Index of Industrial
Production for Aircraft and Parts reached its highest level
in more than 10 years. Although the pace of new orders has
slackened, they were still running well above the level of
shipments through the third quarter. We expect moderate
growth in aircraft production to continue in 1980.

Ordnance   +2.3% in 1979
                                         +1.6% in 1980

Despite recent talk of beefing up our defense posture, there
are no indications in order trends of anything more than small
gains in this industry.

Containers   -.6% in 1979
                                         -1.5% in 1980

Sales of canned beverages have been caught in the squeeze
on discretionary spending as consumers try to maintain their
basic standard of living despite inflation and slow income
growth. Metal can production limped through the last six
months without encouraging prospects for most of 1980. Shipments of barrels, drums and pails are reflecting the economy's
slow slide into recession. Despite these weaknesses, the
container industry has its inventories of finished metal
cans, barrels and drums under control and should be able to
withstand the recession without dramatically cutting production.

##
jr

ECONOMIC INDICATORS

(Dollars in Billions)

(Seasonally Adjusted Annual Rates)	Year 1979	% Chg. 79/78	1980 by Quarters I	II	III	IV	Year 1980	% Chg. 80/79
Gross National Product (Current $)	2363.8	+11.1	2452.8	2499.7	2587.4	2671.4	2552.8	+8.0
Gross National Product (1972 $)	1428.7	+2.1	1406.4	1405.9	1427.9	1447.9	1422.0	-0.5
Consumer Spending	921.8	+2.3	917.3	920.8	934.3	948.9	930.3	+0.9
Private Domestic Investment	215.4	+0.5	191.1	189.1	194.2	204.3	194.7	-9.6
Business Fixed Investment	148.7	+6.1	143.5	138.1	137.4	140.0	139.8	-6.0
Structures	47.6	+8.4	46.3	45.7	44.9	45.0	45.5	-4.4
Equipment	101.1	+5.1	97.2	92.4	92.5	95.0	94.3	-6.7
Change in Business Inventories	10.6	–	-2.0	0.0	+4.5	+6.5	2.2	–
Federal Government	98.9	+0.3	99.0	100.0	102.0	103.5	101.1	+2.2
State & Local Government	174.4	-0.1	172.0	172.9	174.8	176.2	174.0	-0.2
Disposable Personal Income	993.4	+2.1	991.7	996.5	1011.1	1025.8	1006.3	+1.3
Prices								
GNP Price Deflator (1972=100)	165.5	+8.9	174.4	177.8	181.2	184.5	179.5	+8.5
Consumer Price Index (1967=100)*	217.5	+11.3	233.8	239.9	245.7	251.1	242.6	+11.5
Wholesale Price Index (1967=100)	235.6	+12.6	257.1	265.7	273.3	279.3	268.9	+14.1
Corporate Indicators								
After Tax Profits (1972 $)	83.3	+8.2	72.8	66.8	68.4	73.4	70.4	-15.5
Cash Flow (1972 $)	129.0	+4.9	121.7	116.7	117.8	122.9	119.8	-7.1
Compensation per Manhour (1967=100)	253.2	+9.5	270.0	277.4	284.7	293.2	281.3	+11.1
Labor Costs per Unit of Output (1967=100)	214.0	+10.3	228.1	233.3	237.3	242.5	235.3	+10.0

* All Urban Consumers

Economic Research
December 7, 1979

MARKET INDICATORS

(Dollars in Billions)

	Year 1979	% Chg. 79/78	1980 by Quarters				Year 1980	% Chg. 80/79
			I	II	III	IV		
Industrial Production (1967=100)*	151.1	+3.4	144.6	142.8	146.5	149.6	145.9	-3.4
FRB Durable Goods Index (1967=100)	145.3	+4.0	133.5	134.4	139.5	144.1	137.9	-5.1
New Car Sales - Total (000 Units)	10,638	-5.9	2,020	2,560	2,366	2,594	9,540	-10.3
- Domestic (000 Units)	8,350	-10.2	1,586	2,009	1,893	2,101	7,589	-9.1
Domestic Car Production (000 Units)	8,356	-8.9	1,785	1,945	1,608	2,229	7,567	-9.4
Domestic Truck Production (000 Units)	3,111	-16.4	600	625	669	815	2,709	-12.9
Capital Spending – Mfg. (1972 $)*	45.0	+4.9	44.4	42.2	41.8	42.8	42.8	-4.9
Nonresidential Constr. P.I.P. (1972 $)*	65.7	0	63.0	63.2	62.2	61.1	62.4	-5.0
Oil and Gas Footage Drilled (Mil. Ft.)	240.0	+3.7	61.3	61.7	62.5	67.5	253.0	+5.4
Private Housing Starts (000 Units)*	1,719	-14.3	1,330	1,440	1,525	1,660	1,490	-13.3
Factory Appliance Shipments (000 Units)	32,550	-2.0	7,762	8,500	8,200	7,600	32,062	-1.5
FRB Nonelectrical Machinery (1967=100)	162.6	+5.9	150.0	148.3	156.0	153.0	151.8	-6.6
FRB Electrical Equipment (1967=100)	145.8	+7.9	132.7	130.3	131.3	138.7	133.3	-8.6
FRB Agricultural Equipment (1967=100)	145.0	+9.2	143.7	145.1	138.2	138.3	141.3	-2.5

* Seasonally Adjusted

Economic Research
December 7, 1979

STEEL INDUSTRY FORECAST 1980
(thousands of tons)

	Total Domestic Consumption	(+) Exports	Consumer Inventory Change	(-) Imports	(=) U.S. Mill Shipments	Raw Steel Production	Steel Inventories (million tons) Consumer	Mill
Jan.	8,654	225	-800	1,100	6,979	9,600	25.8	18.0
Feb.	8,716	225	-800	1,100	7,041	9,600	25.0	17.9
Mar.	8,886	225	-400	1,250	7,461	10,200	24.6	17.8
I Q	26,256	675	-2,000	3,450	21,481	29,400		
Apr.	8,602	225	-500	1,200	7,127	9,800	24.1	17.9
May	8,867	225	-500	1,300	7,292	10,100	23.6	18.0
June	9,082	225	-300	1,400	7,607	10,600	23.3	18.3
II Q	26,551	675	-1,300	3,900	22,026	30,500		
July	8,712	200	-100	1,450	7,362	10,250	23.2	18.5
Aug.	8,496	200	+100	1,450	7,346	10,100	23.3	18.4
Sept.	9,255	200	0	1,450	8,005	11,100	23.3	18.5
III Q	26,463	600	0	4,350	22,713	31,450		
Oct.	9,436	200	-100	1,450	8,086	11,250	23.2	18.5
Nov.	9,328	175	0	1,450	8,053	11,250	23.2	18.7
Dec.	9,123	175	-100	1,400	7,798	10,750	23.1	19.0
IV Q	27,887	550	-200	4,300	23,937	33,250		
1980	107,157	2,500	-3,500	16,000	90,157	124,600		
1979	114,469	2,802	+600	17,124	100,746	135,599	26.6	18.1
1978	113,906	2,422	+2,742	21,135	97,935	136,689	26.0	19.7
1977	108,059	2,003	+391	19,307	91,147	124,746	23.3	17.7
1976	103,049	2,654	-1,971	14,285	89,447	128,224	22.9	19.7

Economic Research
December 7, 1979

129

V. BUSINESS FORECASTS

19.   The Memphis Economy

(First Tennessee National Corporation)

THE COMPANY: First Tennessee National Corporation is a
                 bank holding company located in Memphis,
                 Tennessee. The company employs 3,381
                 people in its banking operations.

THE REPORT: The success of any business, especially
                 banking, is largely dependent on its man-
                 agers's knowledge of current economic con-
                 ditions and trends on the local, regional,
                 and national levels. This report on the
                 Memphis economy was researched and written
                 so that the officers of First Tennessee
                 National could make more informed decisions
                 about banking transactions in Memphis.

MEMO TO: W. W. Mitchell

FROM: James Zabel

DATE: Friday, June 24, 1977

RE: The Memphis Economy

Introduction:

Except for some seasonal weakness in the financial variables
regularly monitored, most other indicators point to an improving economy here in Memphis and throughout Tennessee. It
appears that, like the national economy, the local and state
economies have encountered no problems in shaking off the
effects of a very severe winter. Indeed, the economy of
Memphis today is much stronger than would have been expected
given the economic statistics of last Autumn.

Unemployment:

The recent declines in the seasonally unadjusted unemployment
rates for the Memphis labor market, for Tennessee, and for
the State's other major metropolitan areas have been nothing
short of dramatic, with declines of a full percentage point
and more common-place. During the January to April interval,
the unemployment rate in Tennessee dropped by 1.7 points; in
Nashville, by 1.5 points; in Memphis, by 1.3 points; and in
Knoxville and Chattanooga, by about one point. Except for
Chattanooga, where the labor market information is not compiled
by survey methods, these declines left April, 1977 unemployment rates 1.5 to 1.9 points lower than April, 1976 rates;
furthermore, these declines placed the unemployment rate in
Tennessee and each of its major metropolitan areas at or below 5.0%, significantly lower than the corresponding national
unemployment rate of 6.9%.

However, at least in Memphis, the improvement in the unemployment rate is resulting from a decline in the civilian labor
force as well as the more customary decline in the number of
unemployed persons. Over the twelve month period May, 1976
through April, 1977, the decrease in the number of unemployed
persons of 4,800 is matched by a decline of 4,900 in the
civilian labor force. The continued reduction in the size of
Memphis' civilian labor force runs completely counter to the
normal cyclical pattern of a growing labor force in a recovering economy.

Also, because the unemployment statistics are not adjusted for
seasonal variation, increases in the unemployment rate for
May and June should be expected. Teenage students will enter
the labor force looking for summer and part-time employment,
causing at least a temporary uptick in the reported employment
rate.

Housing:

The residential construction industry continued to strengthen
in Shelby County in May. Total residential units permitted
during the month equalled 957, down slightly from April's

volume of 1100 units but more than double the units permitted
in May, 1976. Of special significance has been the issuance
of permits once again for new apartment units. In the first
five months of 1977, permits for 1455 new apartment units
were issued compared to none in the first five months of 1976.
Largely because of this renewed activity in apartment construction, permits for 3270 new residential units were issued in
the first five months of 1977, more than double the number
issued in the like period a year ago. But even for single-
family units, permit issuance during the same five month period ran 21 % ahead of a year ago.

Sales of new conventional single-family units and of condominium units have remained brink thus far in 1977. In May,
329 new single-family units were sold, an increase of 11% over
April sales and of 86 % over sales in May, 1976. Sales of
new condominium units totalled 96, an increase of 52 % over
April sales. Compared to the first five months of 1976, sales
of new single-family houses in the January through May period
of 1977 were running ahead almost 41 %, and sales of condominium units were running ahead better than 55 %.

General Business:

Retail sales expanded sharply in March in Tennessee and its four
major urban counties. As in February, increases ranged between
10 % and 15 %, with Davidson and Knox Counties reporting the
largest gains, 16.7 % and 14.5 % respectively. For March, retail sales in Shelby County rose 12.1 %, following a 10.9 %
increase in February. Despite the strength of retail sales in
February and March, the weakness in January sales was so pro-
nounced that, among the four urban counties, only sales in
Davidson County in the first quarter of this year exceeded
sales in the first quarter of 1976. For the entire state,
however, retail sales in the first quarter were up 6.4 % over
sales in the comparable 1976 period.

In Shelby County, new automobile and truck sales picked up in
May after a dip in April, climbing 10.3 %. Compared to May,
1976, monthly registrations of new automobiles and trucks were
5.2 % greater. Through the first five months of this year, new
automobile and truck registrations totalled 21,408 units, about
1000 units (4.4 %) more than the pace of a year ago and more
than 5000 units (32.3 %) ahead of the pace at the depth of the
recession in the first half of 1975.

Activity at Memphis International Airport in May was mixed compared to April. The volume of air express and the number of
air passengers in May showed increases over their April levels
of 6.6 % and 4.7 % respectively; on the other hand, the volumes
of air mail and air freight in May were lower than their April
volumes by 4.7 % and 6.0 % respectively. Compared to the year
earlier levels, all of the indicators exhibited modest increases.

Financial Activity:

Financial indicators continued to drift in Memphis during May
based on data from the three large weekly reporting banks.
Compared to April, demand deposits fell 2.7 % in May; total time
and savings deposits, 0.7%; and total gross loans, 1.0 %. In
part, this weakness reflected normal seasonal patterns, the

second quarter traditionally being the ebb of loan and demand
deposit activity in Memphis. Significantly, deposits this May
were slightly greater than a year ago, and total loan volume
was 6.4 % larger. Again, compared to May, 1976, outstanding
commercial and industrial loans were 9.5 % greater; outstanding
consumer instalment loans were 9.7 % greater; and real estate
loans outstanding were up substantially, 18.8 %. Only agricultural loans were lower; and while the relative decline was large,
25.5 %, the dollar volume of such loans was small, only $15
million out of a gross loan portfolio for the three large banks
of $1410 million.

For the State's other metropolitan areas, the April commercial
banking indicators revealed no clear trends. Member banks in
Knoxville reported a 4.7 % increase in demand deposits during
April, and member banks in Chattanooga showed a 3.3 % increase
in loans outstanding. By and large though, financial activity
was flat. [Because the banking agregates are now being reported
for the standard metropolitan statistical areas rather than the
larger trade and banking areas, consistent year-to-date and
month-over-month comparisions cannot be made.]

For two items, net loans made and acquired and loan commitments,
activity at federally chartered savings and loan associations
in Tennessee, thus far in 1977, has shown impressive gains over
the level of activity in 1976. Loan commitments have consistently exhibited monthly increases ranging from 15 % to 20 % at
the federal S & L's in all of Tennessee as well as in Memphis,
Nashville, and Knoxville; increases over the year earlier
amounts have been even larger, lying in the range of 30 % to
70 %. Increases in net loans made and acquired, on both a
monthly and annual basis of comparision, while more volatile,
have also been large. But net savings flows to these financial
intermediaries have slowed down dramatically. In the first five
months of 1977, the net inflow of savings into federal savings
and loan associations was down from the comparable 1976 period
in Memphis by almost 70 %; across all of Tennessee, by nearly
29 %; and in Nashville, by 16.5 %. In Knoxville net savings
inflows were practically equal for the two periods. In fact in
Memphis, these savings and loan associations experienced net
runoffs in deposits in January, February, and April. These
trends, combined with figures on the behavior of savings and
time deposits at the commercial banks in Tennessee's principal
cities, could be indicating a slowdown in the very rapid
acquisition of liquid assets by households that has been so
conspicuous thus far in the current recovery/expansion.

_____

James Zabel/am

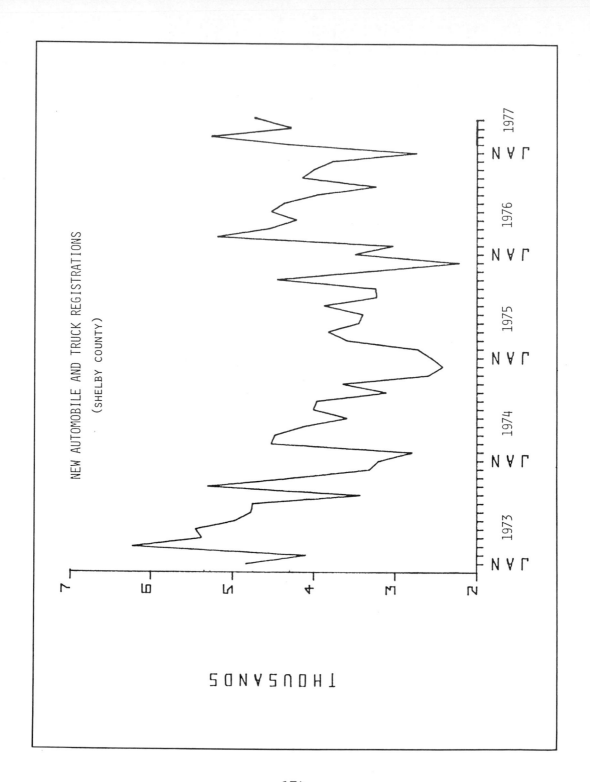

NEW AUTOMOBILE AND TRUCK REGISTRATIONS
(SHELBY COUNTY)

THOUSANDS

134

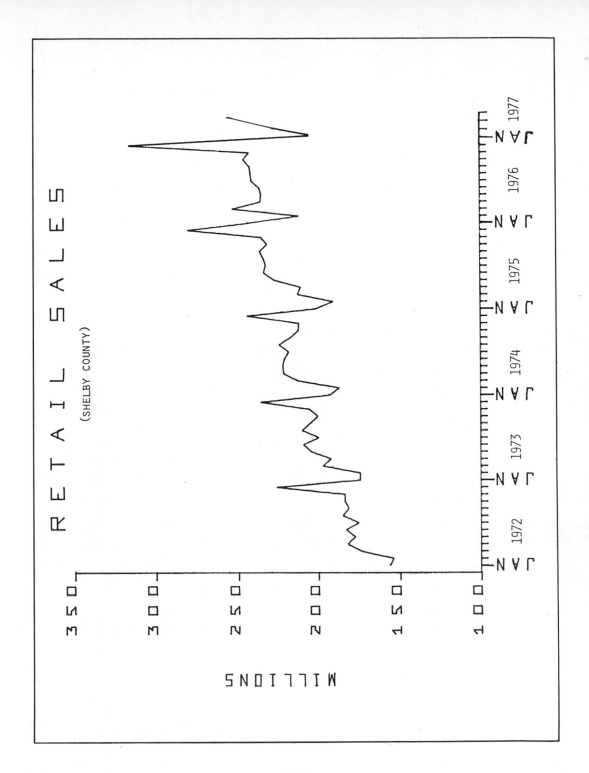

RETAIL SALES

(SHELBY COUNTY)

MILLIONS

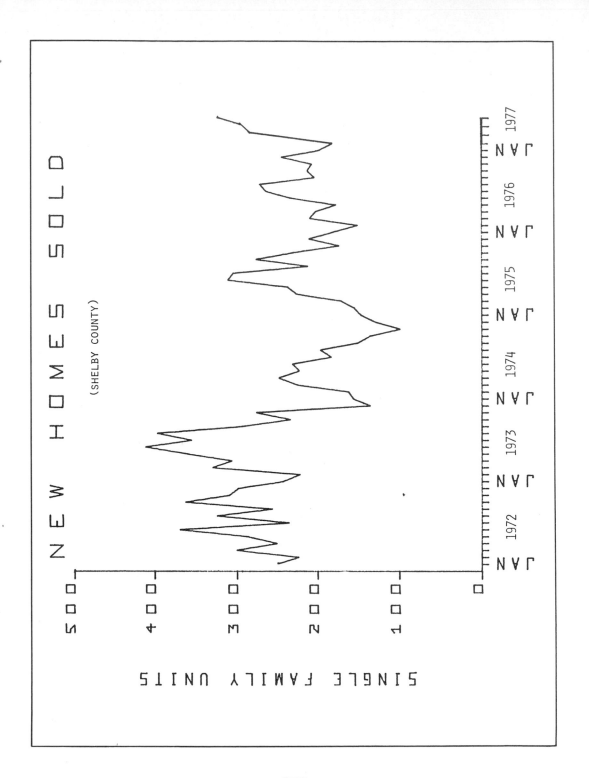

NEW HOMES SOLD

(SHELBY COUNTY)

SINGLE FAMILY UNITS

JAN 1972 JAN 1973 JAN 1974 JAN 1975 JAN 1976 JAN 1977

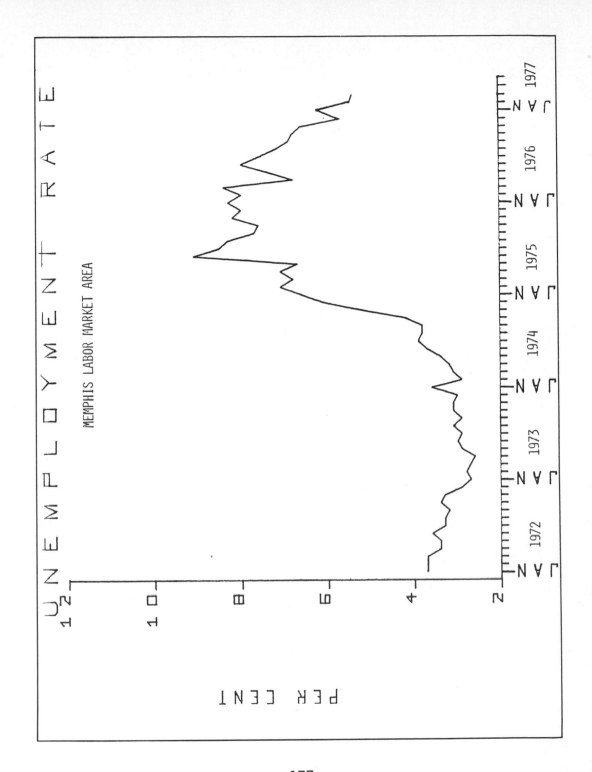

UNEMPLOYMENT RATE

MEMPHIS LABOR MARKET AREA

PER CENT

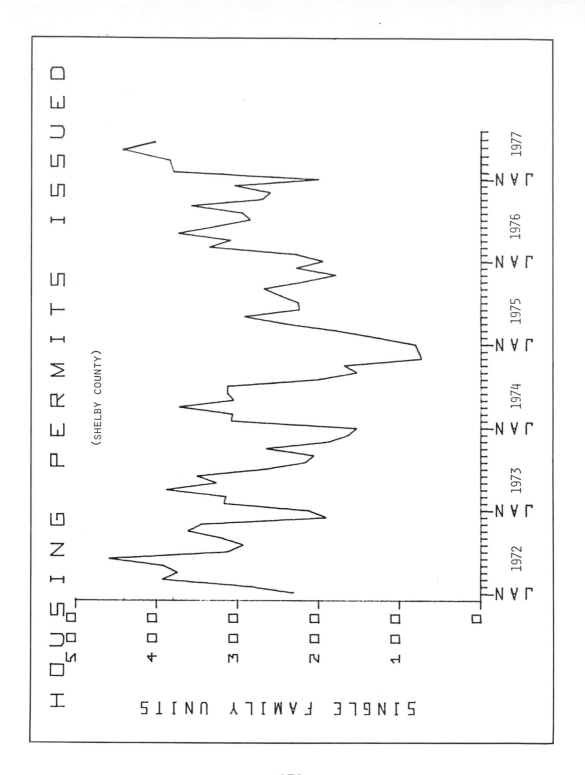

HOUSING PERMITS ISSUED

(SHELBY COUNTY)

SINGLE FAMILY UNITS

VI. REPORTS ON INTERACTION WITH GOVERNMENT

As government regulation of private industry has
escalated in the past decade, corporations have seen
the need to make their reactions to these regulations
known not only directly to members of Congress but
also to their employees and to the general public.
Their willingness to take public stands on governmental intervention has led to the proliferation of a
relatively new kind of report, the "position paper,"
which outlines a company's agreement with and/or ob-
jections to aspects of pending legislation or regulations already in force.

This section contains two "position papers" and
a third information paper written to help company employees better understand a particular legislative
issue.

VI.   REPORTS ON INTERACTION WITH GOVERNMENT

    20.   Solid Waste Disposal

        (Exxon Corporation)

THE COMPANY: The Exxon Corporation produces, refines, transports, and markets various petroleum products and is involved in mining operations through its various subsidiaries and divisions. Corporate headquarters are located in New York, New York. The corporation employs approximately 137,000 people.

THE REPORT: Because it does business in one of the most heavily regulated industries in the nation, Exxon finds occasion to write many "position papers" on regulations and pending legislation that affect its operations. Exxon uses not only a standard stationary format but also a standard organizational pattern ("Background--Position") for all the "position papers" it issues. This standardization allows the reader who must go through many of these reports to do so more quickly and with more understanding.

ENVIRONMENTAL CONSERVATION -- GENERAL		PAGE
		1 of 2
	SECTION	SUBJECT
SOLID WASTE DISPOSAL	V	B-5

Statement of Position

B a c k g r o u n d

The objectives of the Resource Conservation and Recovery Act of 1976 (RCRA) are to promote the protection of health and the environment and to conserve valuable material and resources by, among other things:

1. Regulating the management of hazardous wastes.

2. Prohibiting open dumping of solid wastes.

3. Providing technical assistance to state and local governments for the development of improved solid waste management techniques.

4. Promoting resource conservation and recovery through research and develop-ment programs and cooperative efforts among federal, state, and local governments and private enterprise.

The term "solid waste" is broadly defined by RCRA and includes not only solid discarded material, but also liquids, semisolids, and contained gases in discarded material. A "hazardous waste" is a solid waste which may have significant adverse effects on health or the environment. Wastes generated by Exxon which will be regulated under RCRA include such things as, tank bottoms, cooling tower sludges, spent catalysts, waste oil, API separator sludges, biological sludges, tailings from metals mining, empty drums and containers, and spill clean-up residues.

A major emphasis of RCRA, and Exxon's primary concern with RCRA, is the management of hazardous wastes. The Act requires EPA to promulgate regulations establishing:

1. Criteria for identifying which wastes are hazardous.

2. Standards for generators and transporters of hazardous wastes, including a manifest system which tracks the disposition of hazardous wastes.

3. Standards and a permit system for operations of hazardous waste treatment, storage, and disposal facilities.

A state may be authorized to administer the hazardous waste program provided the state program is essentially equivalent to the federal program.

The regulations and programs implemented under RCRA are expected to have a substan-tial impact (more stringent controls, higher transportation and disposal costs) on the petroleum industry, particularly the refining, and marketing functions. Coal and minerals activities will also be affected significantly.

P o s i t i o n

Exxon recognizes the potential dangers to human health associated with improper handling, storage, and disposal of hazardous wastes. Exxon also recognizes the need to protect the environment from the adverse effects which result from impro-per management of all solid wastes. Accordingly, Exxon believes that nationwide solid waste management is particularly desirable, especially in light of the ever-increasing amounts of waste material being generated by the nation's growth and by the increasing amounts of by-product wastes resulting from air and water pollution controls. Exxon strongly supports cost-effective resource conservation and recovery to reduce the amount of solid waste.

ENVIRONMENTAL CONSERVATION -- GENERAL		PAGE 2 of 2
	SECTION V	SUBJECT B-5
SOLID WASTE DISPOSAL		

Concerning the development of regulations for handling, treatment, and disposal of hazardous wastes and the development of solid waste management guidelines for use by state and local authorities, Exxon believes that:

1. The regulations and guidelines should specify performance requirements rather than mandate use of specific control technology.

2. The regulations and guidelines should call for levels of performance that are reasonably attainable, recognizing that "zero-risk" to health and the environment is unattainable. The levels of performance required should provide benefits which are cost justified on an incremental basis. Regulations which require high-cost, low-benefit controls can have a significant inflationary impact.

3. The criteria for identifying hazardous wastes should realistically establish which wastes pose a substantial present or potential hazard. The regulations for handling, treating, and disposal of hazardous wastes should be consistent with these criteria, i.e., the very stringent handling, treatment, and disposal requirements should be used only for wastes which are a significant hazard. The type of control should also be consistent with the type of hazard involved.

4. Any requirement to upgrade or shut down an existing solid waste disposal facility to meet new requirements must allow an adequate time period to accomplish the necessary modifications or to build a new facility.

5. States should not impose their own regulations which would unduly restrict the interstate movement of hazardous wastes.

The regulation of pits, ponds, and lagoons is a major Exxon concern. Seepage limitations from pits, ponds, and lagoons should be reasonably attainable, taking into account the location of the facility and the potential impact of the seepage on ground water. Very stringent seepage controls should be site-specific and required only for wastes which pose a significant threat to ground water quality.

Although there may be some instances where it is necessary to use extraordinary techniques, such as incineration, to dispose of certain petroleum industry wastes, Exxon believes that a properly located and operated landfill is an environmentally sound procedure for the disposition of most petroleum industry wastes. Exxon also considers landfarming an environmentally sound disposal process for those wastes which respond to biological attenuation.

ISSUED: 07/26/79

142

VI. REPORTS ON INTERACTION WITH GOVERNMENT

21. Horizontal Divestiture

(Marathon Oil Company)

THE COMPANY: With headquaters in Findlay, Ohio, Marathon Oil Company produces crude oil, natural gas, refined petroleum products, and
petrochemicals. The company employs
13,354 people.

THE REPORT: Horizontal divestiture legislation directed
at oil companies would require them to dispose (divest themselves) of all interests
in alternative energy sources. This "Legislative Backgrounder" written by Marathon
describes the issue, presents the arguments
on both sides of the issue, defines the
company's position, and then offers the
facts that support that position. This
pattern, though it appears more informal
than the one used by Exxon, is still a
standard format. (The facts, figures, and
opinions in this report were based on information available at the time the reports
were written.)

Legislative Backgrounder

HD-1
2/8/77

HORIZONTAL DIVESTITURE

The Issue

The issue is whether or not oil and gas producing companies may participate in development of non-petroleum energy resources such as coal, uranium, geothermal steam, oil shale and solar. Proposed legislation would prohibit oil companies from alternative fuel development and require divestiture of their existing non-petroleum energy operations.

Why It's Important

Three-fourths of the nation's energy consumption is in the form of oil and natural gas, but domestic reserves and production of those commodities are declining; and it is estimated that over half of the oil and gas resources in North America have been discovered. If dependency on foreign oil is to be arrested, these other forms of domestic energy must be developed at a vastly increased rate. The oil industry is well equipped technologically, operationally and financially to compete in the total energy field. If it is precluded from doing so, it will have to either gradually liquidate or transfer its resources outside of the energy field as oil and gas operations decline. In either case, the national energy production effort would be deprived of major dedication of capital and technology at a time when it is most needed.

Marathon's Position

Marathon strongly opposes horizontal divestiture because it is anti-competitive and against the public interest. Contrary to the purpose stated in horizontal divestiture bills, it would seriously stifle competition in energy production by arbitrarily prohibiting entry of able competitors. Oil companies would be precluded from competing in other energy forms, and this restriction would be a strong disincentive for others to enter the oil business. Competition in all forms of energy development would suffer. By attempting to cure a presumed monopoly which doesn't exist, horizontal divestiture bills would actually nurture monopoly. And in the bargain, they would divert vast scientific, technological and financial resources from development of all U. S. energy supplies at a time when they are needed the most.

The Other Side

Advocates of horizontal divestiture say that the oil industry is monopolistic and will extend this control to all energy sources if permitted. Horizontally integrated companies would tend to withhold one fuel to bolster the price of another; or withhold all fuel supplies to raise energy prices. They say that even though no case has arisen, current antitrust laws are inadequate to deal with this and that the solution must be a new law.

Public and Government Affairs Division • 539 South Main Street, Findlay, Ohio 45840

Analysis   The attached tables show a striking lack of concentration in
the total energy industry. Uranium oxide production is the only
exception, but concentration in this industry has rapidly declined
over the past twenty years. And, without oil company involvement,
its concentration level would certainly be much higher. Only one
company, Conoco, appears on the lists of the top sixteen energy
producing companies in the three major energy sectors; and it
ranks fourteenth in oil and gas production. Obviously, the oil
industry does not even approach a position in which it could
manipulate prices in other energy forms.

Since the prospects for new domestic oil and gas fields are
diminishing, current reserves are declining and national demand
increasing, alternative fuels must come into the market if we are
to arrest our growing foreign dependency. Absent government controls, these sources will come into use at prices which are
acceptable to both producers and consumers. The task is to get
them developed and not to establish artificial barriers which
will inhibit development, cause needless shortages and increase
prices.

The lack of alternative fuel development to date has been due
largely to poor public policy. The most notable example was
the withering effect on all competing fuels of controlled wellhead prices of natural gas. In the case of coal, capital
requirements for mine safety compliance and high labor costs
compounded the problem. Despite these deterrents, several oil
companies have gone into the coal business, increased the capital
expenditures of failing companies, and registered nearly all of
the coal-related synthetic fuel patents over the past ten years.
Indicative of the industry's contribution to uranium exploration,
it drilled over half of the total exploration footage in 1972
even though representing only 17% of the active exploration companies.

Oil companies have shown the interest and ability to compete in
all energy industries. No evidence of concentration or price
fixing has been shown. Also absent is any rationale why current
antitrust laws would be inadequate to deal with problems of
concentration or price fixing if they should arise.

Most of the prospective coal and uranium land is owned by the
federal government. It thus lies within the government's power
through leasing policies such as acreage limitation to prevent
undue concentration of these resources in a few companies without
resorting to horizontal divestiture.

Legislative
Status

In his campaign, President Carter said, "I support legal
prohibitions against ownership of competing types of
energy -- oil and coal, for instance." On February 6,
Secretary of Interior Andrus announced that he favors
horizontal divestiture. Senator Kennedy, who will chair
the Antitrust and Monopolies Subcommittee, has expressed
particular interest in it. Undoubtedly, there will be a
serious and sustained threat to bring it about and it could
be part of the Administration's energy package.

The most noteworthy House bills introduced are H.R. 683,
Seiberling (D-Ohio) and 30 others, which would call for
complete horizontal and vertical dismemberment of all oil
companies regardless of size and prohibit joint ventures
among large firms; a group of bills which would prohibit
control of alternative energy sources, which includes
H.R. 929, Harrington (D-Mass.) and 14 others; H.R. 93,
Kastenmeier (D-Wis.); H.R. 1664, Eilberg (D-Pa.); and
H.R. 1564, Conte (R-Mass.). The Judiciary Subcommittee
on Monopolies and Commercial Law, Rodino, chairman, will
consider the bills.

On the Senate side, Senators Abourezk and Kennedy are
particularly interested, but no bills had been introduced
as of February 8.

SELECTED INFORMATION ON HORIZONTAL DIVESTITURE

Oil Company Participation in Non-Petroleum Energy Fields

- Not a single one of the top four U. S. crude oil producers rank among the top four U. S. coal producers or the top four U. S. uranium producers.

- Sixteen of the 22 major oil companies are not now producing and delivering coal.

- Seventeen of the 22 major oil companies are not now producing and delivering uranium.

- The leading oil company engaged in uranium production ranks 29th in U. S. crude oil production.

- The leading oil company engaged in coal production ranks 14th in U. S. crude oil production.

- The only U. S. oil company engaged in commercial production of geothermal steam ranks 10th in the U. S. crude oil production.

- The only U. S. oil company engaged in commercial production of tar sands ranks 11th in U. S. crude oil production.

- Only two of the top 22 crude oil producers are presently producing and delivering both coal and uranium.

	U. S. Bituminous Coal & Lignite Production Concentration Ratios %					U. S. Uranium Oxide Production Concentration Ratios %				
	1955	1960	1965	1970	1975	1955	1960	1965	1970	1975
4-Firm	17.8	21.4	26.6	30.7	26.4	79.9	51.4	55.4	55.3	54.3
8-Firm	25.5	30.5	36.3	41.2	36.2	99.1	72.4	79.3	80.8	77.9
15-Firm	34.7	39.7	45.6	52.2	45.9	100.0	94.6	98.1	100.0	NA
20-Firm	39.6	44.5	50.1	56.5	50.6	100.0	99.6	100.0	100.0	100.0

TOP 16 COMPANIES IN EACH ENERGY SOURCE
1974 PRODUCTION

	Crude Oil & Natural Gas [1]	Coal [2]	Uranium [3]
1.	Exxon	Peabody	Anaconda
2.	Texaco	Conoco	Kerr-McGee
3.	Std. of Indiana	Occidental	Utah International
4.	Shell	Amax	United Nuclear
5.	Gulf	Pittston	Exxon
6.	Mobil	U. S. Steel	Union Carbide
7.	Arco	Ashland/Hunt	Rio Algom Mines
8.	Std. of Calif.	Bethlehem	Cotter Corporation
9.	Union	N. American Coal	Conoco
10.	Getty/Skelly	Peter Kiewit	Dawn Mining
11.	Phillips	Sohio	Pioneer Nuclear
12.	Sun	Eastern Gas & Fuel	Homestake Mining
13.	Cities Service	Westmoreland	Western Nuclear
14.	Conoco	Gulf	Atlas
15.	Tenneco	Utah International	Federal Resources
16.	Marathon	American Electric Power Co.	Getty/Skelly

[1] Source: Annual Reports and Statistical Supplements.

[2] Source: Keystone News Bulletin.

[3] Source: Exxon estimate based upon ERDA mill production figures by state, Annual Reports, press releases, and mill capacities reported by ERDA.

VI. REPORTS ON INTERACTION WITH GOVERNMENT

22. [Analysis and Summary of Horizontal
       Divestiture and the Petroleum Industry]

    (Marathon Oil Company)

THE COMPANY: With headquarters in Findlay, Ohio, Mara-
                thon Oil Company produces crude oil, nat-
                ural gas, refined petroleum products, and
                petrochemicals. The company employs
                13,354 people.

THE REPORT: Marathon's continued concern about horizon-
                tal divestiture legislation (see Report #
                21) can be seen in this analysis and sum-
                mary of the book, Horizontal Divestiture
                and the Petroleum Industry. Although most
                of us probably think of book reports as
                purely academic exercises, this memo and
                attachment illustrate that book reports
                can serve a useful purpose in the business
                world when the publications they analyze
                contain information and opinions managers
                think employees should know.

TO _____ Mr. P. J. Kuntz _____ DATE _____ September 30, 1977 _____

OFFICE _____ Room 7209 _____ FROM _____ J. A. Davidson _____

_____ OFFICE _____ Room 7203 _____
(USE THIS LINE FOR FILE REFERENCE OR SUBJECT)

Following is an analysis and summary of *Horizontal Divestiture and the Petroleum Industry* by Jesse W. Markam, Anthony P. Hourihan, and Francis L. Sterling, published by the Ballenger Publishing Company.

Analysis

This book evaluates the desirability and major effects of currently proposed horizontal divestiture legislation on the energy industry and the nation as a whole. The authors applied the standards of workable competition to the energy industry and its various subsectors to determine whether proposed horizontal divestiture would improve the industry's competitive performance. The study is based on comprehensive data, not previously available to the public, obtained from twenty-three large petroleum companies as well as new data from the National Science Foundation, the U. S. Census of Manufacturers, and various business journals.

The authors all have strong business and economic backgrounds. Mr. Markham, an economist and professor at Harvard, has written numerous publications, has taught at several universities, and was Director of the Bureau of Economics of the Federal Trade Commission. Mr. Hourihan has taught at Harvard and is presently working on a Ph.D. in Business Economics there. Mr. Sterling is Vice President of Management Analysis Center, Inc., an international management consulting firm and has consulted numerous domestic and foreign organizations.

The book takes a very organized and in-depth look at the subject. In addition to the usual subjects of concentration levels, market power, financial strengths of the oil companies, and the crossover of technology, the book also looks at such subjects as fuel substitutability, the economic and physical feasibility of playing one fuel against another, and asymmetry in the petroleum industry.

As would be expected, the authors concluded that under any logical test, the arguments for horizontal divestiture cannot be supported, that horizontal divestiture would in many cases create the very conditions its proponents seek to prevent, and that, "... the social costs as measured in terms of prospective lost price competition, capital availability, the development of energy sources, and technological progress may be significant." It goes on to conclude, "... it is apparent that a serious conflict exists between a national policy that on one hand assigns a high priority to the provision of low cost energy supplies to consumers and the accelerated development of energy resources to achieve energy self-sufficiency, while on the other hand seeks large-scale dismemberment of precisely those operations that are most likely to bring these objectives about."

The authors look at each subject of debate on horizontal divestiture beginning
with concentration levels and market power. While noting that no single test
exists, they feel that a four-firm concentration ratio of 50 per cent is a
reasonable level below which tacit collusion is difficult or impossible. Based
on the 1974 data used in the study, the four-firm concentration ratio based on
production for oil producers is 26 per cent; oil and gas producers, 25.1 per
cent; and for companies involved in oil, gas, coal, uranium and geothermal,
only 18.4 per cent. The eight-firm ratio for oil companies is 41.7 per cent,
and even the 20-firm ratio is only 61.4 per cent. As many other studies have
done, these numbers reaffirm the conclusion that there is not enough concentration in the oil or energy industry for tacit collusion to occur.

Oil company behavior in relation to alternative energy sources is heavily
discussed. Pricing, capital investment, R & D, and technology transfer are
subjects often debated when discussing horizontal divestiture. The conclusions on these subjects are:

>   Pricing - Given the structure of the energy industries, no single
>   petroleum company owning either coal or uranium subsidiaries is
>   able to control prices of the various alternative energy sources.
>
>   Capital Investment - In view of potential capital shortages and
>   the huge amounts of risk capital necessary to develop potential
>   future energy sources, the petroleum companies are not only the
>   prime sources but may well be the only potential major private
>   source of these outlays.
>
>   R & D - Research efforts are somewhat enhanced by large firm size;
>   and significant areas of synergy exist between research in various
>   energy resource areas.
>
>   Technology Transfer - There is an actively functioning licensing
>   system within the petroleum industry which encourages effective,
>   efficient R & D, and which moves technology quickly from the
>   patent stage to the commercialization of the more attractive
>   patents. This allows smaller firms access to the modern techno-
>   logy with minimal or no R & D themselves.

Again, these are conclusions brought out by most analysts who have made a
rational examination of the horizontal divestiture issue.

The authors also examined the charge that energy companies could and would
artifically constrain production of one form of energy or another. They
concluded that where demand is increasing more rapidly than available domestic
supply, given the structure of the industry, "it is not to any profit-
maximizing energy firm's advantage to artifically restrict production."
Here again, a rational evaluation leads to a logical conclusion that
horizontal divestiture is not needed and is unwise.

A relatively unheard of topic brought out by the authors is "asymmetry."
The subject of asymmetry in the petroleum industry is an area of little note
in most discussions of horizontal divestiture, probably because of its
rather complex and sophisticated nature. The asymmetry argument and its

Mr. P. J. Kuntz
September 30, 1977
Page 3

implications for public policy are defined as follows: "(1) Asymmetry means dissimilarity between competing firms' assets, organization structures, product lines, business strategies, and objectives. (2) As the degree of asymmetry between competitors increases, the likelihood that they can advantageously pursue an identical joint profit-maximizing form of behavior decreases. Hence, asymmetry reduces the incentive for, and possibility of tacit or overt collusion among competitors." The authors concluded that a considerable degree of asymmetry presently exists among the major petroleum companies and allowing them to continue their diverse paths of horizontal diversification will increase the degree of asymmetry in the energy industry. While not easy to convey to laymen, this is another supporting argument against divestiture.

While the book does make a very thorough study of the horizontal divestiture subject, it is a very complex work. As such, it is probably not easily related to by the layman. It appears to be geared more to those already knowledgeable about the industry or academia. The key points are there, but they are not always easy to grasp.

Attached is a summary which takes a more in-depth look at the key points made by the authors.

JAD:emc
Att.

Horizontal Divestiture and the Petroleum Industry

Summary

Following is a summary of the key comments found in Horizontal Divestiture and the Petroleum Industry.

The book is basically divided into three areas of discussion. First is a discussion of concentration in the energy industry. Second is an analysis of oil company behavior in relation to alternate energy sources. This includes price competition, capital requirements of non-petroleum energy sources, R & D, and technology transfer. The third area deals with the pro-competitive structural aspects of the energy industry or asymmetry.

Concentration in the Energy Industry

The real concentration level of the energy industry and its market power is often a key area of discussion in the horizontal divestiture debate. The authors recognize that there is no single concentration ratio above which competition is absent. The works of several key antitrust scholars such as Eugene Singer, Joe Bain, Carl Kaysen, Donald Turner, and the White House Task Force on Antitrust Policy are noted and discussed. Bain indicates that a four-firm concentration ratio of 76-100% gives a high likelihood of collusion, 51-75% a moderate likelihood, and 26-50% a low likelihood of collusion. Kaysen and Turner advocate market power as occurring when one firm controls 50% or more of the market and/or four firms control 80% of the market. The White House Task Force on Antitrust Policy recommended legislation which assumed a four-firm ratio of 70% was needed for an industry to be concentrated. The authors' use of a four-firm ratio of 50% is, therefore, application of one of the tougher standards used in determining concentration.

Using year end 1974 data from the FTC and other sources, the authors compiled concentration ratio data based on both production and privately controlled reserves in the energy industry and used a BTU equivalent basis for uniformity. The results are:

Concentration Ratios Using Selected Definitions of the Energy
Industry, Based on Production in BTU Equivalents, 1974

		Energy Industry Definition			
Concentration Ratios	Oil	Oil & Gas	Oil & Gas & Coal	Oil & Gas & Coal & Uranium	Oil & Gas & Coal & Uranium & Geothermal
4-firm	26.0%	25.1%	19.1%	18.4%	18.4%
8-firm	41.7	39.2	31.5	29.7	29.7
20-firm	61.4	59.0	49.6	47.8	47.8

Concentration Ratios for Selected Definitions of the Energy
Industry, Based on Privately Controlled Reserves Expressed
in BTU Equivalents, 1975

			Energy Industry Definitions			
Concentration Ratios	Oil	Oil & Gas	Oil & Gas & Coal	Oil & Gas & Coal & Uranium	Oil & Gas & Coal & Uranium & Shale Oil	Oil & Gas & Coal & Uranium & Shale Oil & Geothermal
4-firm	35.1%	29.7%	27.4%	26.7%	23.4%	23.4%
8-firm	54.2	45.6	42.8	41.6	36.6	36.6
20-firm	73.1	67.8	67.8	67.2	62.1	62.1

From these results, the authors conclude that the levels of concentration
in the U. S. energy industry are relatively moderate and not near the cut-off
point above which problems of tacit collusion or monopoly are likely to occur.
They also note that the broader the definition used -- the lower the level
of concentration.

Oil Company Behavior Relative to Alternate Energy Sources

In the area of price competition, the authors note that in order for
energy companies to avoid or circumvent price competition, three criteria
must be present. (1) Various utility fuels must be substitutable. (2) The
economic incentive for "non-arms-length" fuel pricing must be present.
(3) It must be physically possible for producing companies to substitute
one fuel for another. The authors first note that the utility sector
is about the only sector where energy substitutability is feasible to any
degree. Within this sector they note that no new utilities will be allowed
to burn natural gas and only a few will burn oil, and then only when it is
not practicable to burn coal. Thus, recently enacted and proposed regulations
significantly limit the first criteria (product substitutability).

Regarding the economic incentive for "non-arms-length" fuel pricing,
the authors first note that even if one assumes that all oil companies act
as a tight-knit oligopoly, they could not control the price of coal. The
top 20 oil companies only control about 10% of coal production and 30% of
all privately held coal reserves. Thus any action of price stabilization
would only result in non-oil coal producers acquiring the business.

Also noted in this discussion of pricing, is the fact that coal pricing
for the user is primarily dependent upon transportation costs. Of the four
basic alternatives for coal transportation; mine-mouth power plants, barge
movement, slurry pipelines, and rail movement; three of the four are either
partially or completely out of the control of the coal companies. Thus it
is the transportation charges which become the critical factor in determining
the mine mouth price of the coal in most cases, and not the coal companies
themselves. A comparison of Western coal and Persian Gulf crude oil shows
that 75% of the total coal price is transportation while only about 11% of
the cost of crude oil goes for transportation.

In analyzing the physical ability of a single company to substitute one fuel for another, the largest coal companies which are also oil companies are examined. These include Continental (8.6% of the coal market), Occidental (3.5%), Ashland (2.3%), Standard of Ohio (1.6%) and Gulf (1.3%). Looking at Continental, the largest, the authors note that they are primarily a western oil company but an eastern coal company. As a refiner, Continental is primarily oriented toward gasoline instead of heavy utility fuels which might be a substitute for coal. These same type conditions are noted for the other companies, leaving the authors to conclude that in no case are both the oil and the coal company segments of a firm large enough to be considered even possibly dominant firms. They thus conclude that none of the three criteria necessary to avoid price competition exist.

The discussion of capital requirements for nonpetroleum energy sources is based around three possible cases: (1) oil imports continue, (2) oil imports are eliminated by 1990, and (3) oil imports are eliminated by 1985. In 1975 dollars, the capital requirements are estimated to be: (1) oil imports continue: $54.1 billion by 1985, $142.9 billion by 1990; (2) oil imports eliminated by 1990: $113.1 billion by 1985, $325.9 billion by 1990; (3) oil imports eliminated by 1985: $230.5 billion by 1985. The authors note this wide difference in amount, but conclude, at minimum, "capital expenditures in the range of $40 to $50 billion (1975 dollars) must be made over the next ten years to develop nonpetroleum energy sources."

The authors do not project capital availability but they do examine the various industries which are or probably will be most involved in this needed financing, such as utilities, steelmakers, mining companies, independent coal producers, and petroleum companies. Their past expenditures, their financial positions, and their anticipated future needs are all discussed. It is noted that oil industry investment in nonpetroleum energy has been substantial and the authors conclude, "Because petroleum industry capital investment (and thus availability) has historically dwarfed other segments of U. S. manufacturing, to foreclose this source of funds -- could have severe adverse effects on the development of nonpetroleum energy resources."

A significant portion of the book is devoted to a discussion of energy R&D and the transfer of the resulting technology. The authors note that in 1972, 62% of all private energy R&D expenditures were by petroleum companies; and 55% in 1973. They also note that 46% of all coal conversion patents from 1964-1975 were by oil companies and 80% of the oil shale patents in this period were by oil companies. All of the commercial oil shale projects in existence at the time of writing were funded entirely by oil companies. It is brought out that R&D in the coal industry was virtually nonexistent prior to the oil companies' participation and ownership. The authors conclude that oil companies have "significantly promoted the utilization of non-oil technology far above what it otherwise would have been."

Licensing revenues are examined as a method to evaluate the transfer of this oil company generated technology. The authors obtained data from 11 companies of their 23 oil company sample about their revenues from licensing. In 1975 these companies listed total licensing revenues of $125.1 million compared to R&D expenditures of $343.2 million for a revenue to R&D ratio of 36%. From this they conclude technology transfer does exist to a large degree.

The large amount of oil industry technology which can "cross-over" or be applied to other energy segments is noted, especially in oil shale, tar sands, geothermal and coal. This cross-over effect combined with the oil industry's R&D capabilities lead some coal representatives to conclude that, from a technological standpoint, "... it would be a detriment to the coal industry if the oil companies were kept out of the business."

Asymmetry

The discussion of asymmetry is relatively new to the horizontal divesti-ture subject. The book notes that it has previously been confined almost entirely to academic circles. The discussion of asymmetry is based around the idea that the more diverse the various firms' strategies, product lines, assets, objectives, etc., the less likelihood that they can advantageously pursue a collusive or cooperative relationship. Horizontal diversification will in fact increase this asymmetry or difference between firms and decrease any likelihood of collusive behavior. The book compares different pairs of oil comapnies of approximately the same size in terms of sales and notes the wide divergence in strengths and strategies. For example, a comparison of Amerada Hess and Cities Service reveals that Cities is much more involved in natural gas and has sales greatly in excess of refining ability while Amerada Hess has larger refining ability which approximates its sales. It also shows Cities heavily involved in plastics, industrial chemicals and metals while Hess has no interests in any of these products. The authors tie this asymmetry argument into the "freedom-of-entry" discussion and conclude, "Hence, the Horizontal Divestiture Bill will not only have adverse effects on future competitors in the petroleum industry, but in the non-petroleum sectors of the energy industry as well."

JAD:emc

VII. MARKETING REPORTS

Well-researched, clearly written marketing reports are essential tools for the manager who must determine the potential market for new goods and services or choose the most effective method of presenting either new or established products and services to consumers. The highly competitive nature of the marketplace in our economic system places a heavy burden on those who must make marketing decisions; consequently, the reports through which they must present information and express opinions become extremely important.

In this section are examples of reports that gather and analyze information about the marketplace and the consumers in it and one example of a report that presents a marketing strategy.

VII. MARKETING REPORTS

23. Car Maintenance Practices of
    Self-Service Gasoline Customers

24. Motorist Perceptions of Market Place Competition

25. Dealer Feelings and Beliefs About
    the Service Station Business

    (Amoco Oil Company)

THE COMPANY: Amoco Oil Company (Standard Oil Company
                  [Indiana]) produces, refines, transports,
                  and markets petroleum products including
                  gasoline, diesel and jet fuels, motor oils,
                  chemicals, plastics, and fertilizers.
                  Headquartered in Chicago, Illinois, the
                  company employs 47,011 people.

THE REPORTS: The following three reports, researched and
    (3)   prepared by Amoco's Marketing Research De-
                  partment, reflect that company's desire
                  to keep in touch with the practices and
                  opinions of consumers and its service
                  station personnel. The latter group is
                  especially important to the company since
                  it is the segment of the company's market-
                  ing team closest to the consumer.

Marketing Research Department - Amoco Oil Company - Volume V - No. 42 - November 17, 1977

PREVENTIVE MAINTENANCE FREQUENCY CHECKS - SELF-SERVE VS. NON-SELF-SERVE CUSTOMERS

Survey Question: "Consider the newest car in your household. For each of the following, indicate how often (A) you or someone else in your household checks it personally, (B) you have it checked at a service station, and (C) you have it checked at other places (car dealer, repair garage, etc.)."

| | Average Number of Times Checked Per Year | | | | | |
| | (A) Personally | | (B) Service Station | | (C) Car Dealer/ Garage, Etc | | TOTAL | |
Maintenance Check Item	Self-Serve	Non-Self-Serve	Self-Serve	Non-Self-Serve	Self-Serve	Non-Self-Serve	Self-Serve	Non-Self-Serve
Oil level..................	30	22	7	13	1	1	38	36
Water in battery............	16	11	5	7	1	1	22	19
Radiator coolant............	16	11	3	5	1	1	20	17
Air in tires...............	13	10	4	6	1	1	18	17
Transmission fluid..........	8	6	2	3	1	1	11	10
Power steering fluid........	8	5	2	3	1	1	11	9
Fan belts..................	7	5	2	2	1	1	10	8
Brakes.....................	7	5	1	2	1	1	9	8
Radiator hoses.............	7	4	2	2	1	1	10	7
Air cleaner................	5	4	2	2	1	1	8	7

Note: A "Self-Serve Customer" buys from a self-serve station 50 percent or more of the time. A "Non-Self-Serve Customer" buys from a self-serve station 25 percent or less of the time.

IMPLICATIONS. The contention that the growing number of self-serve and gasoline-only facilities will cause more frequent mechanical breakdowns of cars due to a lack of preventive maintenance is not supported by survey research data. The 42% of motorists who buy from self-serve outlets 50% or more of the time are at least as conscientious about preventive maintenance checks as the 58% who buy from self serves 25% of the time or less. As the table shows, the average self-serve buyer checks his own motor oil 30 times a year and has it checked 8 times--a total of 38 checks per year. The average non-self-serve buyer checks his own oil 22 times and has it checked 14 times--a total of 36 times a year. A similar pattern is observed for the other nine maintenance items checked by about 1,400 motorists in September 1977.

Marketing Research Department - Amoco Oil Company - Volume V - No. 1 - January 12, 1977

MOTORISTS ASSESS THE COMPETITIVE CLIMATE IN RETAILING. Just how much competition do motorists perceive within various types of retail businesses? In the October Market Monitoring Survey, we asked more than 1,600 motorist households to rate several different types of retail businesses according to how much or how little competition exists in the areas where they live. The following chart summarizes these ratings:

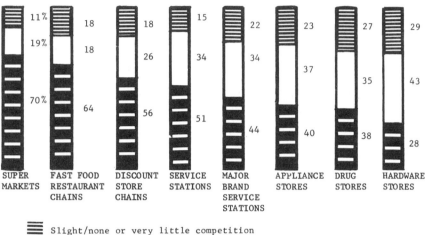

Slight/none or very little competition

Moderate amount of competition

Extremely high/high amount of competition

SERVICE STATIONS ARE SEEN AS COMPETITIVE. The chart shows that the top three competitive businesses in the minds of consumers are supermarkets, fast food restaurant chains, and discount store chains. Service stations in general follow closely with 51% of motorists saying they are either extremely or highly competitive. Then come major brand service stations, appliance stores, and drug stores. Hardware stores are seen as the least competitive of the eight types of retail businesses rated.

IMPLICATIONS. Motorists on the whole see adequate competition among service stations. They feel they have a choice in selecting a brand and a location for buying gasoline and related automotive products and services. The diversity of market offerings by service stations--products, prices, and services--makes for a vigorous competitive climate which is clearly perceived by motorists.

Marketing Research Department - Amoco Oil Company - Volume V - No. 5 - February 11, 1977

STANDARD/AMOCO DEALERS ARE OPTIMISTIC. Although somewhat less optimistic than they were in December 1974, 70% of Standard/Amoco dealers surveyed in December 1976 say they are optimistic about their futures as service station dealers. And two of three say their morale is high (versus 75% in December 1974).

MORE DEALERS SEE SELF SERVES SELLING MOST GASOLINE. The biggest single change in dealer outlook over the past two years reflects the growth of self-serve gasoline marketing. In December 1974, only 24% agreed that self serves would eventually dominate gasoline retailing, and 52% disagreed. Two years later, 39% agree that self serves would take over most gasoline sales, and an identical 39% disagree.

DEALERS ARE LESS SATISFIED WITH SALES AND NET INCOME. As indicated in the table, a second significant change took place over the past two years in dealer satisfaction with sales and net income. In 1974, 28% said

STANDARD/AMOCO DEALER FEELINGS AND OPINIONS ABOUT THE SERVICE STATION BUSINESS

PERSONAL FEELINGS/GOALS/CONVICTIONS	Percent Agreeing 12/76	12/74	Change
"I'm glad I'm a service station dealer"..................	83	87	-4
"I 'live and breathe' the service station business"........	67	65	+2
"I would like to take things easier in my business"........	50	46	+4
"I sometimes feel overwhelmed by my business"..............	47	46	+1
"I'm satisfied with my present sales and income"...........	23	28	-5
BUSINESS SUCCESS PREDICTORS			
"In the service station business, if you don't grow, you'll die"...	79	78	+1
"A dealer who can sell his gasoline customers their tire replacement needs will be a successful dealer"...........	67	70	-3
THE SHAPE OF THE FUTURE			
"Oil companies couldn't run service stations without lessee dealers"...	60	63	-3
"Eventually, most gasoline will be sold through self-service outlets"..	39	24	+15
VIEWS ON GOVERNMENT AND BUSINESS			
"Dealers should support oil company efforts against more government control"....................................	66	66	nc
"Service stations doing repair work should have certified mechanics"...	62	62	nc
"Major oil companies should be controlled more by the government"..	8	10	-2

☐ Boxed changes are statistically significant

they were satisfied with their present sales and income, and 53% said they were dissatisfied. In 1976, the percent satisfied fell to 23% and the percent dissatisfied rose to 55%--a net change of seven percentage points.

DEALERS CONTINUE TO SUPPORT OIL COMPANY RESISTANCE TO MORE GOVERNMENT CONTROLS. Two of three Standard/Amoco dealers continue to agree with this statement: "Dealers should support oil company efforts against more government control." Only 13% disagree compared with 17% in 1974.

DEALERS LIKE THE SERVICE STATION BUSINESS. Although down slightly since 1974--87% to 83%--the overwhelming majority of Standard/Amoco dealers agrees, "I'm glad I'm a service station dealer!"

VII. MARKETING REPORTS

26.   Comparative Financial Analysis

(Birmingham Trust National Bank)

THE COMPANY: Birmingham Trust National Bank's operations
                   are centered in Birmingham, Alabama. The
                   company employs approximately 1,100 people
                   in its offices and banks in that area.

THE REPORT: For any company to market its products or
                   services successfully, it must regularly
                   and candidly assess its strengths and weak-
                   nesses in the marketplace. This report is
                   a realistic appraisal of its relative posi-
                   tion among the four leading banks in its
                   market by Birmingham Trust National Bank.

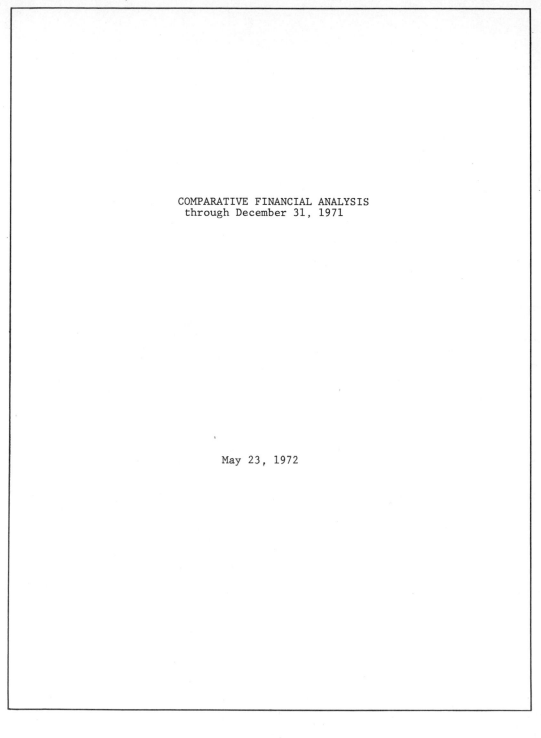

COMPARATIVE FINANCIAL ANALYSIS
through December 31, 1971

May 23, 1972

Introduction

The purpose of this report is to provide a financial
analysis of the four largest banks in Birmingham. However,
the primary emphasis is concentrated on a comparison of the
Birmingham Trust National Bank and the First National Bank
with some commentary on areas where the Exchange Security Bank
and the Central Bank have affected either the Birmingham Trust
or the First National. This report is designed to provide a
financial background on the above banks as well as a basis for
future comparisons between the Birmingham Trust and its principle
competitors. By providing such an analysis, an insight into both
BTNB's strengths and weaknesses can be focused upon so that the
former can be exploited and the latter can be reduced.

Growth Rates and Ratios of Financial Data

The total period analyzed in this section is the nine year
span from 1963-1971 with a four year period from 1963-1966
and a five year period from 1967-1971 also analyzed. By a
close examination of the growth rates, one can determine past
trends as well as obtain a possible insight into the future
performance of BTNB and its competitors.

In each of the growth categories analyzed for the Birmingham
Trust, it becomes evident that the period of greatest growth
came between 1963 and 1966. The 1967-1971 period had a considerably smaller growth rate, but undoubtedly the former period
was heavily influenced by the Bank For Savings merger with BTNB.
Nevertheless, one of the most dramatic reductions in the compounded growth rates came in the loan category whereby from
1967-1971 the growth rate was 7.60% as compared to 16.00% growth
from 1963-1966. However, the First National Bank managed a small
increase in their loan growth to 6.85% versus the earlier period's
6.00% rate. Asset and deposit growth also slowed moderately in
the 1967-1971 period while First National managed a small increase in growth for assets and suffered a small decreased growth
rate in deposits. It is important at this point to emphasize that
whereby our growth rates may have slowed, our absolute figures are

2

considerably larger in 1971 than in 1967 and that it becomes
harder to maintain a high level of growth as an organization
becomes larger. Nevertheless, in spite of this point, the First
National Bank improved its position, however slight, between
1967-1971. Consequently, it is possible to conclude that in so
far as assets, deposits, and loans are concerned, the rapid growth
of Exchange Security and Central Bank has competitively hurt the
Birmingham Trust and the First National. An examination of the
growth rate figures in the quantitative section of this report will
substantiate this conclusion.

Eventhough growth rates for BTNB have been hurt by its two
smaller competitors, the ratio of loans to deposits for BTNB is
far ahead of First National and compared favorably with Exchange
and Central. However, the ratio of reserve for loan losses to
book value is substatially higher for BTNB than its competitors
which represents a more conservative statement of earnings. Generally, the more conservative the accounting practices a firm has,
the higher the quality of the resulting earnings.

Two more growth items that were carefully analyzed were gross
revenues and operating expenses. This area has some of the
brightest performances of BTNB and offers some of the most optimistic prospects for the future despite a few weaknesses in some
trends.

Before actually discussing the growth rate of gross revenues
for the Birmingham banks, several ratios involving gross revenues
will be examined. Without exception, BTNB out performs its city
rivals in the rate of return of gross revenues to assets, and to
deposits, as well as the rate of return of loan income to loans
and investment income to investments. This performance extended
throughout the time period covered in this report. In addition,
BTNB, to date, has actually increased its lead since 1962 over
First National in every category. At the same time, BTNB has
generally held its own against Exchange and Central. Consequently, it can be said that the Birmingham Trust is earning
a larger relative rate of return on the above items in so far as
gross revenues are concerned. The record of this performance
has been so consistent through the years that there appears to
be no reason why a similar performance would not continue for at
least the near future.

In examining the growth rates for gross revenues and for
operating expenses, it was decided that a better trend involving
the financial data could be obtained if the major components of
the gross revenue and the expense items were analyzed. This was
only done for BTNB and First National.

2

In the period 1963-1966, operating expenses grew faster than revenues by a compounded rate of 3% for BTNB and by a similar amount for First National. The major contributor to BTNB's revenue growth both absolutely and relatively was the interest and fee on loan item which grew at a 23% rate, The principle expense item was the 25.50% growth in interest on deposits. Again the First National had a very similar performance, except that our growth rates were very much higher in both revenues and expenses. For example, BTNB's growth rate in salaries and benefits was better than two to one over First National's rate.

In addition, the difference between the growth rate of the revenue from loans and the interest on deposits was 2.50% in favor of interest on deposits while the First National's interest on deposit item grew better than 9% faster than the loan income. Basically, however, from 1963-1966 BTNB had a better performance in revenue growth than the First National while the latter controlled its growth in expenses better than BTNB.

In the next period analyzed from 1967-1971, BTNB's gross revenue growth slowed sharpely because loan income growth declined to 12% from 23%. However, growth in total operating expenses also declined sharply to 13.50% from 21%. The reason for this good trend was a dramatic decline in the growth of salaries and benefits and in the growth rate of interest on deposits. This good trend was partially offset by a surge in occupancy and rental expenses and "other" expenses which grew faster than the "other" income category. Furthermore, it is important to note that our net operating income before security gains or losses also declined eventhough the difference between the growth rates of revenues and expenses were favorably narrowed. An explanation for this apparent paradox is that there are different basis from which growth is calculated such that if total revenues grow at a faster pace, net earnings will have a similar performance eventhough the margin of expenses might grow faster than revenues. In addition, the period 1967-1971 is different in general from 1963-1966 because of the Bank For Savings merger. Finally, as our net earnings' growth has slowed, it is not a surprise that growth in capital also slowed since one of the basic components of capital is undivided profits which changed as profits change.

The First National Bank also had some significant changes between 1967 and 1971. Their gross revenue growth increased as a result of a sharp increase in the "other" income category and in spite of a large decline in the growth of the investment income. However, First National also had an increase in the growth of operating expenses whereas BTNB's expense growth declined very significantly. In fact, the margin of growth between revenues and expenses widened such that First National's net earnings growth

declined albeit relatively less than ours. The reason for the
growth in their expenses can be attributed to a surge in salaries
and benefits and "other" expenses. for the first time in the
nine year period analyzed, First National's expense growth was larger
than BTNB's.

To briefly summarize some of the above principle conslusions,
it can be said that although revenue growth, net earnings growth, and
capital growth slowed between 1967 and 1971, BTNB's expense growth
also declined. This decline in expenses can be directly traced to
a smaller growth in salaries and benefits. Yet, BTNB's "other"
income item did not grow as fast as its counterpart of "other"
expenses. In addition, it can be said that BTNB has been hurt
competitively by Exchange Security and Central in so far as loan,
deposit and asset growth is concerned. Undoubtedly, there is some
significant distortion in the true growth pattern as a result
the merger of BTNB and the Bank For Savings for much of the growth
between 1963-1966 came in the first year of the merger.

Conclusions concerning First National's performance center
primarily around the fact that they have held their own between
1967-1971 against Exchange and Central in relation to the 1963-
1966 period where their growth performance was somewhat less.
However, First National's growth in expenses is trending upward
and from the viewpoint of an investor, it is very likely that
their expenses might grow even faster in the next few years as
their computer capacity is expanded and as greater centralization
of branches occurs. BTNB has already completed the major part of
their expenditures in this area whereas First National has a
significant portion of this expense ahead of them. As a result,
BTNB should reap the benefits of their investment in technological
advances sooner than its competitors such that revenues should
experience good growth while growth in expenses should some under
tighter control.

Balance Sheet Analysis

The balance sheet figures were computed as a percentage of
total assets for the purpose of isolating significant shifts in
the composition of the asset and the liability figures.

In analyzing the asset section of the balance sheet, it

becomes readily apparent that BTNB and its competitors are keeping a smaller percentage of their assets in cash and due from items. Basically, this represents an attempt to utilize resources to the fullest of their earning power and to have as few idle resources as possible.

Another broad trend since 1962 is the shift in the bond portfolios away from Federal government securities to an increased share of State, County and Municipal bonds. Again, the banks are striving for greater return on their investments as well as a lessening of tax responsibilities. However, the total percentage of assests invested in all types of bonds has generally declined. The most notable bank in this area is BTNB which had a decline from approximately 27% of assets in bonds in 1962 to approximately 19% of assets in bonds by the end of 1971.

The chief beneficiary from the declines in cash and bond percentages has been the percentage of assets invested in loans. The loan percentage for all the banks has been on a steady upward trend as banks strive for an increased return on assets.

One final item of significance concerning BTNB's assets is the significantly larger portion of assets invested in Federal funds sold as compared to the other banks. This discrepancy becomes most apparent in the years 1970 and 1971. Even if this figure is netted with the Federal funds pruchased, the net figure remains generally larger. Whereas there are probably logical explanations for the above, it is notable that BTNB is the exception among its competitors such that BTNB could be preparing for a surge in loan growth. If such a loan growth should develop, BTNB would be in a liquid enough position to fully participate in this growth.

In so far as buildings and equipment items are concerned, no one bank appears to be in a significantly better positon than the others.

The second major category of balance sheet figures are the liabilities of an organization. The most significant trend in this area concerns deposits. All of the banks analyzed have had a continuing relative shift toward more time deposits and consequently there are relatively fewer demand deposits. This changing relationship is also supported by the absolute figures of the above items. The trend to an increasing share of time deposits does not appear to be abaiting for in the first four months of 1972, demand deposits of BTNB grew at an 11% rate and time deposits grew at a 16% rate. Figures for 1972 on the other banks are not available, but there is little reason to doubt that a similar trend would not also be occuring for these firms.

The other significant liability figure that warrants some
attention is the percent of unearned income. Again BTNB has a
higher figure than its competitors which can be traced to the
type of loans that are made. BTNB has a large consumer loan volume whereby this type of loan is discounted which adds to the
unearned income figure. In addition, BTNB has had a tendency to
discount a larger percentage of single payment loans than its
competitors. Furthermore, discounted notes have a higher yield
than other types of loans such that the loan income to the amount
of loans should be higher. Indeed, this is the case as was noted
earlier in this report whereby BTNB has had for a number of years
a higher loan yield than its competitors.

The third major section of a balance sheet involves the
capital structure of a firm. Basically, BTNB, Exchange Security,
and Central have similar percentages of capital to total assets.
The exception in this category is the First National Bank which
has a relatively larger amount of capital than its competitors.
From the depositors' viewpoint, this characteristic allows the
First National to more easily absorb any losses and acts as a
buffer for any seasonal fluctuations in cash flow. However, the
cost of retained earnings for a bank is higher than the cost of
deposits. Consequently, it can be said from an owner's point of
view that BTNB, with its smaller capital base, is more leveraged
than First National because BTNB uses a larger percentage of
depositors' money for loans and investments at less cost than the
cost of retained earnings. Yet, a smaller capital base does not
allow for as much buffer between seasonal cash flows or loan
losses.

The reserve for loan item and the funds borrowed item have
been discussed earlier in this report.

Operating Income and Expenses

Many of the significant areas involved with the income and
expense figures have been analyzed in the growth and ratio section
of this report. However, there are several areas yet to be covered
that are very important.

One area of importance concerning the operating income half

of the Income Statement concerns the interest and fees on loan
figure. BTNB has consistently had a larger portion of its total
operating income derived from loan income than its competitors.
Since loans yield a higher return than bond investments, BTNB
has certainly been more progressive in striving towards greater
profitability than its competitors. The trend toward greater
reliance on loan income and less reliance on bond income is also
true of the other banks analyzed.

The components of operating expenses and their growth have
already been covered in an earlier section, but the area of net
operating results needs to be explored further for it is in this
area that the greatest amount of weakness concerning BTNB was found
in relation to its competitors.

The percentage of income before taxes and security changes
for BTNB has consistently been very much less than the other banks.
In fact, First National is the leader in this area and has often
had a margin of two to one over BTNB as a percentage of total income.
In addition, First National has led its competitors in the item of
net income before security gains or losses as a percent of total
income. As a result, First National's net income in the same relationship has been first in these categories. BTNB has been consistently last. These findings are further supported by the ratio
comparisons of net operating income before security changes to
various denominators. In each area, First National is the leader
and BTNB is last.

As stated in the introduction of this report, the purpose of
this analysis is not only to look at historical data but to examine the data for possible trends. Therefore, this section of the
report can be ended on a note of optimism in that the trend of
income and expenses since 1962 is favoring BTNB while slowly
running against its competitors. BTNB's growth in expenses has
been slowing while the rate of return of net operating
before security charges to both deposits and assets has been trending
upward. This trend can be observed by an examination of both the
ratio comparisons and the Statement of Income figures. If the
trend continues, BTNB should continue to become more profitable.

One final area of importance is the amount of reinvestment of
net earnings into the operations of the firm. BTNB has generally
reinvested between 55%-65% of its earnings into the bank while
First National has generally maintained a payout ratio of 50%.
Consequently, BTNB has expanded its earnings at a greater pace
from internal reinvestment than the First National Bank. As a
resut, BTNB's stockholder's equity portion of undivided profits
has expanded faster. Yet, as explained earlier, retained earnings
have a cost, and a firm should only retain that portion of its

earnings that can be invested at a higher return than the cost
of those funds. If a firm cannot reinvest its earnings at a higher
return than its owners, then presumably the dividends paid out
should be near 100% of net income. Very few firms are in this
category with the exception of some utilities.

Conclusions and Future Prospects

The French writer and philosopher, La Rochefoucauld, said
that "The greatest of all gifts is the power to estimate things
at their true worth." This report has attempted to do just that
by using the quantitative portion of the analysis to examine not
only the historical data but to indicate possible trends for the
future. In a brief summarization, it has been concluded that
BTNB is number one in its ability to generate gross income from
its various investments in loans and securities. An examination
of both the growth rate figures and the ratio figures support
this conclusion.

It was also found that BTNB is number four in its ability
to take the gross income generated and transform it into a relative position of being number one in its net income results. Yet,
it was found that BTNB is making positive gains in this area whereas, its competitors are losing some aground. (See accompanying charts)

In so far as the future is concerned, the holding company
concept dominates the possibilities of potential change. It should
be very interesting indeed to observe the financial performance
of the four banks analyzed in this report as they begin to operate
and change under the holding company concept. Future financial
results should provide evidence to determine whether the new,
expanded role of banks will be more profitable than the past, more
limited role of banks.

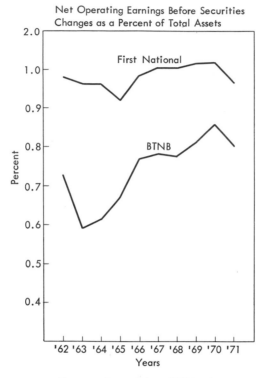

Net Operating Earnings Before Securities Changes as a Percent of Total Assets

The overall trend since 1963 has been upward despite the Bank for Savings Merger. The basic effect of the merger was to hurt short term profitability while at the same time increasing the asset, deposit, and loan base of the combined company.

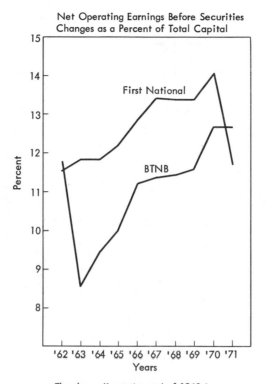

Net Operating Earnings Before Securities
Changes as a Percent of Total Capital

First National

BTNB

Percent

'62 '63 '64 '65 '66 '67 '68 '69 '70 '71
Years

The sharp dip at the end of 1963 is
again attributed to the Bank for Savings
Merger. Since 1963, BTNB's trend has
been steadily moving upward.

Income Before Taxes and Security Changes
as a Percent of Total Operating Income
(Profit Margin)

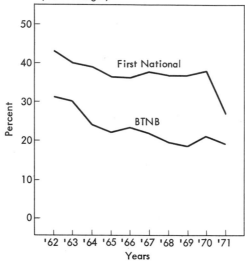

The dip between 1963 and 1964
is attributed to the Bank for
Savings Merger.

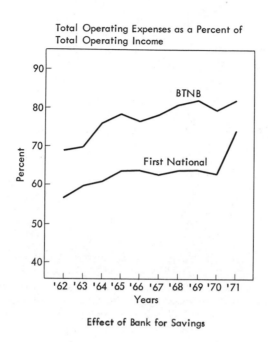

Total Operating Expenses as a Percent of
Total Operating Income

Effect of Bank for Savings

VII.　MARKETING REPORTS

27.　1978 Communications Plan--Consumer Products

(Pennwalt Corporation)

THE COMPANY:　With headquarters in Philadelphia, Pennsylvania, Pennwalt Corporation produces a wide variety of organic and inorganic chemicals, household products, and machinery for commercial and domestic uses.　The company employs approximately 13,900 people.

THE REPORT:　This report outlines a communications plan designed to promote a new line of commercial grade kitchenware cleaning and sanitizing chemicals for Pennwalt.　Note the candid assessment of the difficulties Pennwalt expects to encounter in this new market and the techniques it plans to employ to surmount those obstacles.

1978 COMMUNICATIONS PLAN

DEPARTMENT/DIVISION <u>Chemical Specialties</u> Div.   DATE SUBMITTED <u>March 1, 1978</u>

SEGMENT <u>Consumer Products (Foodservice Market)</u>   PREPARED BY _____

BUDGET CODE # _____   APPROVED   _____

    _____

SITUATION ANALYSIS

This plan outlines promotional activity in support of Pennwalt's entry into the foodservice market with a line of kitchenware cleaning and sanitizing chemicals. That line includes the following products:

    Heavy-Duty, Granular MACHINE WAREWASHING DETERGENT
    Granular MANUAL WASHING DETERGENT
    Liquid MACHINE WAREWASHING DETERGENT
    Fine China WAREWASHING DETERGENT
    Concentrated LIQUID CLEANER
    Liquid OVEN, GRILL & HOOD CLEANER
    BK®-LFI IODINE-BASED GERMICIDE-SANITIZER
    Liquid PRE-SOAK & DETARNISHING AGENT
    GLASS, TILE & COUNTER CLEANER
    LIMESTONE SOLVENT/ACID CLEANER
    WAREWASHING RINSE AID
    Super Active Liquid HAND SOAP

This plan covers only a six-month time frame, representing the introduction period for this new line. Period will extend from May 15th through November 15th, 1978.

TARGET PRODUCT/MARKET SEGMENT CAMPAIGNS

The following market segments will receive advertising/promotional/sales support in 1978 - aimed at major buying influences as indicated:

1. <u>Channels of Distribution</u>

    a. <u>Brokers</u> Principals and end-user sales personnel.

        Support program to consist of sales and training aids/brochures. Efforts to sell distributors and/or end-users will be supported by brand/product awareness advertising directed at foodservice distributors as well as end-users.

b. <u>Distributors</u> Sales managers, buyers and end-user men.

To be supplied, via broker, with sales/product literature.

2. <u>Operators</u> - i.e. end-users

Initial programs to be aimed directly at key buyers of volume accounts in pre-selected areas.

a. commercial chains-fast food and sit-down

b. colleges/universities

c. contract feeders

d. hospitals/nursing homes

e. hotels

FOODSERVICE MARKET SEGMENT

Communications Obstacles & Opportunities

Obstacles

1. Market is characterized by numerous national marketers with the same or similar product line. Pennwalt's entry will offer nothing new in this respect.

2. In several regional markets and trading areas the foodservice chemical business is dominated by small local chemical companies that offer stiff price competition to national marketers.

3. Kitchenware cleaning chemicals and sanitizer products, with respect to pricing, are characterized as being an "auction" type situation with distributors always seeking the best deal from various suppliers prior to committing on purchase. Heavy dealing off list price is fairly common -- anywhere between 7-15% is considered normal.

4. Service, in the form of field representatives solving clean-up and machine problems for end-users, has traditionally been a major benefit offered by national marketers (DiBous, Economics Labs, Wyandotte). No doubt a portion of this market will always demand (or be willing to pay for) this service. Pennwalt will not offer end-user service with respect to chemicals or equipment.

5. Pennwalt will sell through a national network of foodservice brokers -- all totally unfamiliar with the technical and/or service aspect of this product line. Brokers, in-turn will be selling to distributors whose salesmen, for the most part, will be unfamiliar with chemical cleaners and will find it uncomfortable to discuss the line with prospective customers without at least a thorough grounding in the basics.

Opportunities

1. More and more distributors are opting to establish themselves as one-
    stop shopping operations for the foodservice customer. Chemicals are
    an area which traditionally was not handled in this fashion. Moreover,
    the service aspect is either minimized or taken over by the distributor
    himself.

2. It is anticipated that the tremendous growth of the foodservice industry
    will spur merger and consolidation among the nation's 2,900 foodservice
    distributors. It is anticipated that their larger operations will seek
    arrangements with those chemical suppliers offering; (a) technical ex-
    pertise, (b) product uniformity and (c) national distribution.

3. Our entry into this business does not represent a venture into a "new"
    technology for Pennwalt. Technical expertise is available.

COMMUNICATIONS OBJECTIVES

1. Positioning:

    a. To position Pennwalt's line of cleaning and sanitizing chemcials as
        quality products; uniform, tested and proven in the marketplace; that
        the Pennwalt products are produced by one of the nation's largest,
        most responsible, reputable chemical companies.

    b. To position Pennwalt's line of cleaning and sanitizing chemicals as a
        logical extension into a growing foodservice market - an extension that
        has its roots in the food processing, beverage and dairy maintenance
        field.

2. Distributors:

    a. Motivate distributor salesmen to sell the line to target levels by end
        of six-month introductory phase. Program will provide for incentives
        for end-user men.

3. Distributors/Brokers:

    a. To provide both distributor and broker end-user men with sifficient in-depth product knowledge to enable them to demonstrate the Pennwalt line in face-to-face selling.

4. **Advertising:**

   a. To build awareness of the Pennwalt name and products among foodservice distributors and operators in the test market.

5. **Creative:**

   a. To position Pennwalt as a large chemical supplier to the food processing and beverage industry; expertise which is now being brought to foodservice.

   b. To position products as effective and easy to use -- that there are no better at any price under any label.

6. **Promotion:**

   a. To establish in the minds of distributors that Pennwalt is a serious, experienced chemical supplier willing to work out innovative promotions designed to move products.

7. **Sales Training:**

   a. To convince distributors that Pennwalt brokers can and will sell the end-user market.

   b. To convince distributors that Pennwalt/Broker personnel can effectively demonstrate to and train distributor end-user sales personnel.

COMMUNICATIONS STRATEGIES

1. **Advertising:** To utilize regional (zip code circulation) of the key industry distributor and end-user publications during introductory period.

   a. To position this advertising so that it will give maximum exposure to company/products.

   b. To obtain trial of products.

2. **Creative**: Design ads (special inserts) that will work (a) well with regional editions and (b) double as pages 2 - 3 of a 4-page sales brochure.

3. **Promotion**:

    a. Distributor introductory program

        (1) Introductory allowance

            (a) For the "House"

            (b) For the end-user salesman

            (c) Salesman's contest (sweepstakes)

        (2) End-user rebate or "one free with..." program

FOODSERVICE MARKET

KICK-OFF DATE May 15, 1978

TERMINATION & REVIEW DATE November 15, 1978

ACTIVITY	LINE OPERATING INPUT REQUIRED	DATE	ROUTE FOR APPROVAL	COMPLETION DATE	RESPONSIBILITY	BUDGET
7711 PUBLICITY						
01 Pennwalt Entrance	Copy outline approval	4/1	4/7	4/15	G70, K83	
02 Product Line	Copy outline approval	4/1	4/7	4/15		
03 Dist. Training	Lead provided	8/1	9/1	9/15		
04 Program Application	Lead provided	9/1	9/21	10/15		
7713 SPACE ADVERTISING						
Distributor						
01 Foodservice Dist. Salesman	2 pg. insert 4 color		May Issue / June Issue			
End-Users						
01 Institutions/Volume Feeding Mgmt	2 pg. insert 4 color		May Issue / June Issue			
02 Nation's Restaurant News			June Issue Only			
03 Food Equipment & Product News			July Issue Only			
7715 SPACE PREPARATION						
01 Intro New Foodservice Product Line	Preparation and printing of 4 page (blank front & Back) insert Copy platform preparation	3/15	3/21	4/7	G70, K83	

183

CAMPAIGN PLANNING SCHEDULE - PRODUCT/MARKET SEGMENT

FOODSERVICE MARKET

KICK-OFF DATE: May 15, 1978

TERMINATION & REVIEW DATE: November 15, 1978

ACTIVITY	LINE OPERATING INPUT REQUIRED	DATE	ROUTE FOR APPROVAL	COMPLETION DATE	RESPONSIBILITY	BUDGET
7716 DIRECT MAIL						
01 Intro. Kits to Broker Reps.	Prepare outline of material along with introductory deals	3/15	4/1	5/1	G70, K83	
02 Intro. Kits to Distributors	Prepare outline of material along with introductory deals	3/15	4/1	5/1	G70, K83	
03 Direct Mailhouse Charges						
7719 LITERATURE						
01 Data Sheets (12)	Final Copy & Technical Review	4/1	4/15	5/1	G70, K83	
02 Intro. Brochure 4 page, full color	Pick up insert ad for center section - finalize intro offers	4/1	4/15	5/1	G70, K83	
03 Distributor salesman's product Guide	Prepare copy platform and application information on each product	4/21	5/15	6/15	G70, K83	
7729 CONTESTS/SWEEPSTAKES						
01 Dist. Salesmen Contest	Salesmen selling his first order becomes eligible for sweepstake drawing for cash prize $1,000	Begins 5/15	4/15	Ends 8/15	G70, K83	

ACTIVITY	LINE OPERATING INPUT REQUIRED	DATE	ROUTE FOR APPROVAL	COMPLETION DATE	RESPONSIBILITY	BUDGET
7752 CONTAINER & DISPENSING EQUIPMENT						
01 Label & Shipping label copy for 12 products	(Note: No advertising budget figure will be established for this action. Cost will be allocated by operating department under another expense account. Advertising will assist line operating in supervising design and preparation of labels through Purchasing Department.)			4/15	G70, K83	
7758 TRADE PROMOTIONS INCENTIVE PAYMENTS						
01 Incentive payment to distributor salesmen	50¢ per case allowance for distributor salesmen	Begins 5/15		Ends 8/15	G70, K83	
7759 TRADE PROMOTIONS						
01 End-user $5.00 Rebate	Rebate to end-users for the purchase of the first five cases of any combination of Pennwalt products	Begins 6/1		End Offer 10/1	G70, K83	
02 Intro. Allowance	16% off invoice introductory allowance	Begins 5/15		End Offer 8/15	G70, K83	

VIII. AUDIT REPORTS

"I'm in accounting--I'll never have to write reports." This section's reports should reveal how mistaken this typical notion is. Reports written by accountants, usually called audit reports, are among the most important written in or for any company. They must always be clear and precise, but often also require a diplomatic touch.

Audit reports are evaluations of how each unit within a company handles any records that pertain in any way to the flow of a company's assets (e.g. inventory, expenditures, personnel records, purchasing procedures, payroll, etc.). Thus audit reports, whether done by a company's own internal audit department or by an external accounting firm, are an invaluable means of determining which operations are efficient and which operations need improvement. The need for diplomacy obviously comes in the second kind of situations because in them the internal auditor must tell someone he or she wishes to keep as a compatible colleague and the external auditor must tell someone he or she wishes to keep as a client that the procedures being used are not the best or even a good way of operating.

The reports included in this section were written by both external and internal auditors. Notice the blend of precise, clear presentation of information with tactful criticism.

VIII. AUDIT REPORTS

28. & 29.   [Commentary Reports]

(Deloitte Haskins & Sells)

THE COMPANY: Deloitte Haskins & Sells is one of the
                major international accounting firms. The
                reports reproduced here were provided by
                the partners in Deloitte Haskins & Sells's
                office in Houston, Texas.

THE REPORTS: The two reports that follow are examples
     (2)   of what Deloitte Haskins & Sells calls
                "commentary reports." These reports are
                prepared after the firm's accountants have
                audited a company's books and are a series
                of observations about strengths and weak-
                nesses in operating and/or accounting pro-
                cedures and suggestions about how they
                might be corrected. (The names of the com-
                panies being audited have been deleted.)

188

**Deloitte
Haskins+Sells**

1200 Travis
Houston, Texas 77002
(713) 651-1700
Telex 762840

January 23, 1979

Houston, Texas

Dear Sirs:

We have examined the financial statements of
                              for the period ended
November 30, 1978 and have issued our report thereon dated
January 23, 1979. As a part of our examination, we made a
study and evaluation of the Venture's system of internal
accounting control to the extent we considered necessary to
evaluate the system as required by generally accepted auditing
standards. Under these standards, the purposes of such evaluation are to establish a basis for reliance on the system of
internal accounting control in determining the nature, timing,
and extent of other auditing procedures that are necessary for
expressing an opinion on the financial statements and to
assist the auditor in planning and performing his examination
of the financial statements.

The objective of and inherent limitations on any system of
internal accounting control are described in the Appendix to
this report.

Our examination of the financial statements made in accordance with generally accepted auditing standards, including
the study and evaluation of the Venture's system of internal
accounting control for the period ended November 30, 1978,
that was made for the purposes set forth in the first paragraph of this report, would not necessarily disclose all
weaknesses in the system because it was based on selective
tests of accounting records and related data. However, such
study and evaluation disclosed the following conditions that
we believe to be material weaknesses, for which corrective
action may be practicable in the circumstances.

Cash Receipts

The person who handles credit card receipts for the purpose
of preparing the bank deposits also posts the credit card
receipts, tests the Daily Reports received from the Inns, and
makes journal entries to record such receipts.

We recommend that another person prepare the bank deposits
for credit card receipts.

Cash Disbursements

The person who authorizes all capital expenditures also signs the checks for such expenditures.

We recommend that another person sign checks for capital expenditures.

Journal Entries

Checks are signed singly by a person who also makes journal entries to the general ledger.

We recommend that checks be signed by two persons.

In addition to the material weaknesses indicated above, we noted the following conditions which warrant your attention:

Cash

Bank statements were not reconciled to the general ledger during the period ended November 30, 1978, but were reconciled to amounts which the Venture thought the balances should be. Such amounts differed significantly from the general ledger and an audit reclassification of approximately $74,000 was required at November 30, 1978.

Our findings and constructive comments were orally communicated to the Vice-President of Vista Management, Inc. during the audit. We commend you for prompt action in instituting our recommendations.

. The payroll account had not been reconciled since June 1978.

We recommend that the Venture prepare current bank reconciliations for all cash accounts and that adjustments determined in the reconciling process be recorded in the general ledger.

. Currently, the Venture has no procedure to examine paid checks for any unusual features such as alterations, unauthorized signatures, or questionable endorsements.

We recommend that checks returned with bank statements be examined, on a test basis, for unusual or questionable features.

Inventories

. Inventories are priced at the most recent vendor invoice price, regardless if quantities on hand exceed the receipts associated with those invoices.

- 2 -

For a better first-in, first-out valuation, we recommend that quantities on hand which exceed receipts shown on the most recent vendor invoice be matched to and priced using the next preceding vendor invoice.

Accounts Payable

Extensions and additions on vendor invoices have not always been checked by personnel at the Inns or in Houston. Invoices from produce vendors appeared to have many errors in extensions and additions.

We recommend that extensions and additions be checked before vendor invoices are paid and that a procedure be instituted to implement accountability for such checking, such as initialling the invoice or some similar method.

Duplicate payments of vendor invoices are sometimes made.

We recommend that the Venture institute procedures to prevent such duplicate payments.

Accrued Liabilities

Accruals for utility bills are currently being made in three different accounts (Nos. 217-03, 217-10, and 201).

We recommend that all accruals for similar goods or services be made in one account.

Purchases

The Venture has not adopted written purchase order procedures, and relies on oral communication of orders to vendors.

As a control device, we recommend that sequentially pre-numbered purchase orders should be written for all significant purchases. The numbering system should provide a means of identifying the department from which the purchase originates. Purchase orders should indicate approval by an authorized person. Once the vendor's invoice is received, price and quantity should be compared to the purchase order, and any differences investigated.

Payroll Expense

Manual adjustments to the gross pay of salaried employees are sometimes made by the Innkeeper without adequate documentation of the reasons for such adjustments.

We recommend, in order to verify pay adjustments for salaried employees, that the Innkeeper should always record overtime hours or make notation of other reasons for such adjustments.

- 3 -

Telephone Expense

.   Allocations of telephone expense between local service
    costs, long distance costs, equipment costs, and income
    from commissions on long distance calls are not made on
    a consistent basis. For example, directory advertising
    charges are sometimes charged to advertising expense, and
    sometimes included in long distance calls expense.

    We recommend that a standard journal entry to record
    telephone expenses be developed, and that any unnecessary
    general ledger accounts be eliminated.

Housekeeper's Report and Room Revenue Report

.   The Venture has experienced problems in training the Inns'
    personnel to adequately complete the Housekeeper's Report
    and Room Revenue Report. These problems are augmented by
    personnel turnover at the Inns.

    We compliment the Venture for its efforts to overcome
    these problems and encourage continued attention in this
    area. Additionally, we recommend the following:

    .. Implement the use of standardized Maid's Reports and
        retain such reports at the Inns.

    .. Insist that the Night Auditor's room status report be
        reconciled to the Housekeeper's room status report.

General

.   The Venture is to be complimented for implementing
    standardized journal entries. However, it was noted that
    use of a standard numbering system for the journal entries
    has not been developed.

    We recommend implementation of a standard numbering system
    for journal entries to facilitate recognition of the type
    of entry and control over journal entries.

.   Journal entries for both the Venture and
        are filed in the same binder.

    We recommend that journal entries for the two entities be
    filed separately to prevent confusion
                    * * * * * * *
The foregoing conditions were considered in determining the
nature, timing, and extent of audit tests to be applied in
our examination of the financial statements, and this report
of such conditions does not modify our report dated
January 23, 1979 on such financial statements.

We would be pleased to discuss these comments and recommendations with you in greater detail.

Yours truly,

                    - 4 -

INTERNAL ACCOUNTING CONTROL

The objective of internal accounting control is to provide reasonable, but not absolute, assurance as to the safeguarding of assets against loss from unauthorized use or disposition, and the reliability of financial records for preparing financial statements and maintaining accountability for assets. The concept of reasonable assurance recognizes that the cost of a system of internal accounting control should not exceed the benefits derived and also recognizes that the evaluation of these factors necessarily requires estimates and judgments by management.

There are inherent limitations that should be recognized in considering the potential effectiveness of any system of internal accounting control. In the performance of most control procedures, errors can result from misunderstanding of instructions, mistakes of judgment, carelessness, or other personal factors. Control procedures whose effectiveness depends upon segregation of duties can be circumvented by collusion. Similarly, control procedures can be circumvented intentionally by management either with respect to the execution and recording of transactions or with respect to the estimates and judgments required in the preparation of financial statements. Further, projection of any evaluation of internal accounting control to future periods is subject to the risk that the procedures may become inadequate because of changes in conditions and that the degree of compliance with the procedures may deteriorate.

Deloitte
Haskins+Sells

1200 Travis
Houston, Texas 77002
(713) 651-1700
Telex 762840

Board of Governors   September 7, 1979

Houston, Texas

We are submitting to you our Management Report containing our
findings and recommendations concerning internal controls and
other matters resulting from our examination of the financial
statements of the
for the eighteen months ended June 30, 1979. Our report consists
of a series of comments arranged by subject areas as
listed in the accompanying table of contents.

Our findings and recommendations are not the result of a
special study and do not purport to be other than observations incidental to our examination. This report is further
subject to the limitations stated in the Appendix and should
be read in that context.

When comparing our management letter of last year with this
one, you will notice that we have changed the format of presenting our findings and recommendations. Our intent is to
present the comments in a concise manner for your ease of
review without any sacrifice of content. If you desire
additional information about any comment, we can easily
provide it for you.

We have noted significant improvements in the
accounting systems and records since our last examination and
encourage the   to continue that record of progress in
implementing its new accounting system.

We would be pleased to discuss these recommendations with you
and assist the   in their implementation at your request.

Yours truly,

TABLE OF CONTENTS

A. CASH

Finding: Cash recorded on the books was not adjusted for
reconciling items noted during the preparation of bank
reconciliations.

Discussion: Bank reconciliations, particularly for the payroll account, contain items such as voided checks whch should
be corrected in the accounting records on a timely basis.

Recommendation: Items appearing on bank reconciliations should
be investigated and accounting records adjusted where appropriate.
We suggest that the employee who prepares bank reconciliations
also be assigned the responsibility for following up on such
matters and preparing required adjustments.

Finding: Checks have remained outstanding for several months.

Recommendation: We suggest that the responsibility for
investigating old outstanding checks be given to the employee
who prepares bank reconciliations and that stop payments be
issued on lost checks. Also, consider depositing earnings of
clients working in the workshop directly to their trust accounts.

B. EXPENDITURE DOCUMENTATION

Finding: Contracts, bid proposals, job specification reports
and financing agreements are filled in various locations.

Recommendation: We believe that a more efficient filing system
would be to maintain all the documentation pertaining to each
job in one place. Responsibility for maintaining such files,
for major expenditures, could be assigned to one person as an
added control.

C. LEASES

Finding: The   began leasing automobiles and a forklift
during 1979.

Discussion: Generally accepted accounting principles require
that items acquired under lease agreements which are essentially
purchase and financing arrangements ("capital leases") be accounted
for as capital purchases and that the corresponding lease obligation
be recorded as a liability. The lease of a forklift in 1979 met
the specifications of a capital lease.

Recommendation: Management of the   should analyze the
accounting requirements of FASB Statement No. 13 - Accounting
for Leases during the evaluation of alternate methods of financing
the acquisition of property. We would be pleased to assist the
          with such analyses as such occasions arise.

D. PERSONNEL RECORDS

Finding: Personnel files for some employees did not contain employment applications. Also, documentation for salary changes was
missing from some personnel files.

- 3 -

Discussion: Papers are placed in personnel files without being attached to the folder and without being arranged in a standarized manner. Such procedures increase the possibility of documents being misplaced, and make it more difficult to recognize when documents are missing.

Recommendation: Consider the use of a standard index for personnel records and attach all documents to the folders.

E. PAYROLL

Finding: The calculations of daily rates for salaried employees being docked for absences or being paid for additional hours worked were prepared in an inconsistent manner.

Discussion: The different methods, which give different results, used in calculating daily payrates which we noticed were:

(a) Monthly pay times twelve months divided by 260 work days per year.

(b) Monthly pay divided by twenty work days per month.

Recommendation: We suggest that one method be adopted and applied consistently.

F. PROPERTY

Finding: The detail property records have not been updated since 1974 and no physical inventory of property has been taken.

Recommendation: We suggest that the   continuously update the property records and periodically perform a physical inventory of property in order to improve accountability over capital expenditures.

G. RESIDENTS' TRUST ACCOUNTS

Finding: Cash held by the   in trust for residents is deposited in a demand account which earns no interest.

Recommendation: Evaluate the propriety of depositing cash held in trust to an interest bearing account.

Finding: Counselors occasionally make withdrawals from trust accounts for residents who are away from the Residence Hall during the hours the bank is in operation. The withdrawal request is signed by the resident.

Recommendation: Consider assigning an employee, who has no trust account duties, the task of periodically verifying that the residents received cash withdrawn on their behalf by counselors. This employee might also discreetly determine the amount of cash held by various residents. Residents holding excessive amounts of cash could be advised of the possibility of loss or theft.

REPORT LIMITATIONS

We have examined the financial statements of
for the eighteen months ended
June 30, 1979 and have issued our report thereon dated
September 7, 1979. As a part of our examination, we made
studies and evaluations of the   systems of internal
accounting control to the extent we considered necessary to
evaluate the systems as required by generally accepted auditing standards. Under these standards, the purposes of such
evaluations are to establish a basis for reliances on the
systems of internal accounting control in determining the
nature, timing, and extent of other auditing procedures that
are necessary for expressing an opinion on the financial
statements and to assist the auditor in planning and performing his examination of the financial statments.

The objective of internal accounting control is to provide
reasonable, but not absolute, assurance as to the safeguarding of assets against loss from unauthorized use or disposition, and the reliability of financial records for preparing
financial statements and maintaining accountability for
assets. The concept of reasonable assurance recognizes that
the cost of a system of internal accounting control should
not exceed the benefits derived and also recognizes that the
evaluation of these factors necessarily requires estimates
and judgments by management.

There are inherent limitations that should be recognized in
considering the potential effectiveness of any sytem of
internal accounting control. In the performance of most
control procedures, errors can result from misunderstanding
of instructions, mistakes in judgment, carelessness, or
other personal factors. Control procedures whose effectiveness depends upon segregation of duties can be circumvented
by collusion. Similarly, control procedures can be circumvented intentionally by management either with respect to
the execution and recording of transactions or with respect
to the estimates and judgments required in the preparation
of financial statements. Further, projection of any evaluation of internal accounting control to future periods is
subject to the risk that the procedures may become inadequate
because of changes in conditions and that the degree of compliance with the procedures may deteriorate.

Our examination of the financial statements made in accordance with generally accepted auditing standards, including
the studies and evaluations of the   systems of
internal accounting control for the eighteen months ended
June 30, 1979, that were made for the purposes set forth in
the first paragraph of this Appendix, would not necessarily
disclose all weaknesses in the systems because they were
based on selective tests of the accounting records and
related data.

VIII. AUDIT REPORTS

30.   Cands Lumber Division

(The Chesapeake Corporation of Virginia)

THE COMPANY: With headquarters in West Point, Virginia, The Chesapeake Corporation of Virginia produces a wide variety of wood products including lumber, plywood, pulp, paper, and paper and corrugated containers. It employs 2,150 people.

THE REPORT: Although yearly external audits of most firms' financial operations are required by law, most companies maintain an internal audit unit which monitors, in a more intimate way than external auditors can, the company's operations. The following audit report is Chesapeake Corporation's internal auditor's analysis of the operations of one of that company's divisions, Cands Lumber.

TO: The Audit Committee of The Board of Directors

FROM: Internal Auditor

DATE: June 1, 1977

AUDIT OF: Cands Lumber Division

SCOPE

We have recently completed an audit of Cands Lumber Division. Our audit
consisted of a review and documentation of existing procedures and testing
of these procedures as we considered necessary.

EVALUATION

Generally, procedures are adequate for proper managerial and accounting
control. The staff knows the procedures and why a particular task is
performed. There are written procedures or job descriptions covering all
activities we examined. There is some weakness in internal controls from
the lack of separation of duties. This appears to be unavoidable because
of a small staff. This weakness, in our opinion, is offset by the intense
managerial control exercised by the general manager at Cands and by wood-
lands and accounting at West Point.

FINDINGS AND RECOMMENDATIONS

Sale of Logs

The current method of recording the shipment of logs too large for Cands to
process does not provide adequate means to insure payment for all shipments.
Certain elements of control do exist. A sequentially numbered slip is used
to record weight of shipments. However, in our tests we could not account
for all tickets. Additionally, some shipments leave the plant without
tickets after office hours, but while the production area is open. This was
evidenced by payments for more shipments than the weight tickets indicated.

We recommend that all shipments be weighed, that the weight tickets be recorded in a journal numerically, and that the journal be marked to indicate
payment for each shipment.

Payment for Logs Purchased

In our tests of payment for logs purchased, we found adequate separation of duties, extremely accurate clerical computations, and proper recording of transactions in the accounting records.

We recommend that log pricing sheets be dated and signed by the plant manager if a change in the price of logs occurs.

Follow-up of Payroll Audit

In following up on our recent hourly payroll audit, we found that the employee's Withholding Allowance Ceritficates (W-4) which were not on hand in West Point were being obtained from current employees with the current distribution of paychecks.

Purchasing

In our review of purchase orders and invoice processing, we noted that a method had been recently introduced to prevent possible duplication of payment of invoices, where shipment of ordered goods had been split.

In this method, the invoice for the first portion of the shipment was held until the invoice for the subsequent shipment arrived. We suggested that a photocopy of the invoice be retained and the original invoice be processed to prevent possible late payment or loss of discount.

Production Reporting

We reviewed the production reporting system. There appeared to be sufficient production information generated and statistics computed to enable management to be appraised of production status at any time. Where appropriate, we agreed production data to information from other systems and to the financial records. There were no significant variations.

In our review of the data, we noted that underrun percent and the amount of chip-n-saw downtime appeared to be high up through the 4th period. These appear to have been improved in the 5th period.

Lumber Sales

We reviewed the lumber sales invoicing and reporting systems and tested these to the underlying records and to the general ledger. We found no exceptions.

<u>Other Items</u>

We reviewed and tested on a limited basis the cash receipts and payroll
systems. The cash receipts system is presently being modified to a lock
box system. The payroll system appears to be adequately controlled.

by_____

cc: L. H. Camp
     A. H. Eubank, Jr.
     T. G. Harris
     W. J. Phipps
     W. C. Ware, Coopers and Lybrand

IX.   PERSONNEL MANAGEMENT & EMPLOYEE RELATIONS REPORTS

Among the reports grouped in this section you
will find reports that could logically be included in
many of the other sections of this collection. For
example, you will see here reports that outline procedures, request information, present information,
and solve problems. These different "types" of reports are brought together in this section because
in this case report "type" is not as important as report "subject"--people and their jobs.

Jobs are important to people not only because
they provide a means of livelihood but also because
they make a significant contribution to each person's
sense of identity and self-worth; therefore, reports
that deal with people and their work must be written
with special care and sensitivity. This special consideration is an obvious requirement for those reports that will go directly to employees; however, it
is also important in personnel reports that most employees will never see because the tone established
in them can easily filter through a company and influence, either positively or negatively, the attitudes of many employees. The impersonal realities
that often must be a major part of decisions about
personnel matters must be tempered by a consideration
of the human needs of the people involved.

The six reports in this section demonstrate the
concern most businesses have for their most important
resource--people.

IX.   PERSONNEL MANAGEMENT & EMPLOYEE RELATIONS REPORTS

      31.   1976-77 Corporate Recruitment Study

             (Anonymous)

THE COMPANY: This report was provided by a major U.S.
                  manufacturing company with headquarters
                  in a large midwestern city. (The names of
                  the company and the cities mentioned in
                  the report have been changed at the re-
                  quest of the contributing company.)

THE REPORT: If you are a typical student, one of your
                  primary worries right now centers on get-
                  a good job offer when you graduate; con-
                  sequently, you may not have considered
                  that those people on the other side of the
                  process, the company officers responsible
                  for recruiting good employees, also worry
                  about the hiring procedure and are contin-
                  ually reassessing their methods in an at-
                  tempt to get the best people to accept
                  jobs with the company. The following re-
                  port is a summary for general distribution
                  of a very detailed report which analyzes
                  the reasons job candidates accept or re-
                  ject job offers.

204

THE COMPANY

1976-77 CORPORATE RECRUITMENT STUDY

SUMMARY REPORT*

Prepared by: Associate Psychologist, Psychological Services

Background and Purpose

The continued renewal and improvement of the Company's human resource base
through our recruiting efforts is one of the corporation's most vital functions.
Yet, very little information has been available concerning the reasons candidates
for positions throughout the company accept or reject the Company's employment
offers. This study was undertaken to fill this information gap. More specifically, the study addressed the following three questions:

 ·1. What major factors influence job candidates to accept or reject
      Company job offers?

  2. Can we accurately predict job candidates' decisions regarding our
      job offers based upon information gained before the offers are
      extended? This ability would permit us to intervene in those
      cases when highly rated candidates seem likely to reject the job
      offer.

  3. What sources of information regarding the Company do job candidates
      rely upon when making their employment decisions?

Method

    All individuals interviewed at the Headquarters Office, the Research &
Development Lab, and manufacturing plants between late November, 1976 and
May 31, 1977 were invited to respond to a questionnaire specifically designed
for this study. Participants in the study were asked to compare the Company with
competing job opportunities in terms of both their objective characteristics
(such as pay) and their subjective images. They were additionally asked to describe their own self-image and to rate the importance of several potential sources
of information concerning the Company. Responses were received from 218 individuals, representing 51% of all persons interviewed at those locations during that
time period. Both experienced and inexperienced job candidates as well as candidates for all major corporate departments were represented in the sample. In
addition, 42 of these individuals agreed to respond to the questionnaire a second
time, following their job offer decision, thereby permitting a before-after comparison. Among these 42 individuals were 28 persons accepting positions with
the Company and 14 persons taking positions with other firms.

. . . Continued

* A more detailed, technical report is available from Psychological Services.

THE COMPANY

Summary of Major Findings

1. <u>Question 1: Job Decision Factors</u> (reference Tables 1, 2, & 3)

   - The job/organizational chracteristics most frequently used by job candidates to compare the Company with competing job opportunities are the following (in decreasing order of use): (Table 1)

     > Work Climate (e.g., co-workers, autonomy, formality, cooperation)
     > Advancement Opportunity
     > Career Development (including training)
     > Salary
     > Location
     > Varied and Interesting Work
     > Benefits
     > Responsibility and Challange
     > Growth and/or Stability of Company
     > Skills-job Match

   - In all of the above ten areas, more job candidates believed that there are no differences between the Company and other firms than those that believed such differences do exist.   (Table 1)

   - <u>Location</u> is the only area in which job candidates were as likely to describe the Company as worse than the competition as they were to describe the Company as better than the competition (Table 1). Location is also the characteristic in which the Company is most frequently described as worse than the competition. In fact, this location problem appears to be even more acute when one examines the candidates' opinions immediately following their on-site interviews, with Plant 1 suffering most from this negative perception (Table 2). The sole consolation regarding the location factor is that it is perceived as the least valued organizational factor and can be compensated for by other, more valued characteristics (Column 1, Table 1).

   - <u>Experienced</u> <u>and</u> <u>inexperienced</u> job candidates could be distinguished by their beliefs in only four areas. The experienced candidates were more likely to believe that the Company's benefits, work climate, and skills-job match are better than the competitions' while the inexperienced were more likely to believe that our location is better. (Table 3)

   - Some <u>departmental</u> <u>differences</u> were also found. (The following comparisons were limited to those four departments with 25 or more job candidates in the study.) (Table 3)

     Job candidates for Corporate Engineering were most likely (in comparison with research and development cost, manufacturing plants) to believe that the Company's benefits are better than other firms but least likely to believe that there is responsibility and challenge in the job.

. . . Continued

THE COMPANY

Job candidates for Research & Development were most likely to believe
that the Company's work climate and salary are better than other firms,
but least likely to believe that there is a good job-skills match.
Job candidates for Manufacturing were the least likely to believe that
the Company's salary, benefits, company growth and stability, and
career development are better than competing job opportunities. Job
candidates for one manufacturing plant were the most likely to believe
that advancement opportunity, responsibility and challange, and job-skills
match are better than competing firms, while least likely to believe
that the company's location is better.

2. Question 2: Predicting Job Offer Decisions

Approximately 70% of the accept or reject decisions were correctly predicted using questionnaire responses made by job candidates immediately
following their on-site interviews. This level of accuracy is significantly greater than the 50% level one could expect to achieve through
random guessing.

Four sets of imformation were used to achieve this level of accuracy:
(1) a combination of each individual's beliefs and attitudes toward
specific organizational characteristics; (2) the Company's image as
an action-oriented, risk-taking organization; (3) each individual's
self-image as a "considerate" person; and (4) each individual's self-
image as a "flexible" person.

3. Question 3: Important Sources of Information (reference Table 4)

The on-site interviewer(s) is by far the most important source of
information for the Company job candidate, with an average rating
between "highly" and "extremely" important. The remaining five information sources were rated substantially lower, all falling between
"slightly" and "moderately" important. It is worth noting that three
of the top four rated sources are company based: on-site interviewer(s),
company publications, and campus recruiter.

. . . Continued

THE COMPANY

Conclusions and Recommendations

-1- Most job candidates believe that the Company does not significantly
differ from other firms in the major areas of comparison. Consequently,
the company's primary recruitment task is one of differentiating ourselves from the "crowd" rather than overcoming negative beliefs (with
the exception of "location").

The recommended approach for doing so is to concentrate on those organizational chracteristics which are most highly valued by job candidates.
Thus, our "sales effort" should emphasize work climate (i.e., autonomy,
cooperativeness among employees, the friendliness and competency of co-
workers, etc.), the responsibility and challenge associated with work,
as well as its varied and interesting nature, and the advancement and
career development opportunities that exist at the Company. This is
not to say, however, that the other factors, such as pay and benefits
should be ignored. It is simply a matter of where the emphasis should
be placed during conversations with prospective employees.

-2- Location has been identified as our most pervasive problem area. Admit-
tedly, location is not given as much weight by candidates as the other
considerations described in the previous paragraph. Yet, due to the
fact that a large proportion of job candidates perceive the Company
to be very similar to other firms in those more important areas, location is probably a decisive factor more often than we would like it to
be. For this reason, it is recommended that location be singled out
for special attention, especially at Headquarters City and Plant #1 City.

The fact that Headquarters City's image among the national populace
is a negative one is well-known. It is safe to assume, therefore, that
the negative beliefs and attitudes held by job candidates concerning
the city were brought with them. The solution is to bring facts to
their attention that will counter these preconceived notions without
being obtrusive in doing so. To determine how this should best be
done may require the services of an outside consultant. In any case,
the following suggestions merit further consideration. First, the
Recruitment Office should send printed material regarding Headquarters
City to job candidates prior to their visit, rather than waiting to
distribute them during the visit. This suggestion is made with the
expectation that the candidates would be more likely to read the material
if it were not just one of many items given them to read during their
visit. This material could include such items as the Headquarters City
Magazine's "Visitor's Guide to Headquarters City" which is presently being
distributed). In fact, a special packet of materials like that prepared
by a local bank (also available in the Corporate Recruitment Office)
would be an ideal approach. Second, the Company should present a brief,
professionally developed film highlighting the many assets of life in
Headquarters City. The actual content of the film could be developed
based on comments obtained from recent arrivals to Headquarters City.
Moreover, since the "Headquarters City problem" is shared by other local

. . . Continued

firms, the creation of the film could be a joint venture, thereby substantially lowering the development costs for the Company. <u>Finally</u>,
we must not ignore that this study has shown that on-site interviewers
are the most important source of information for the job candidates.
The remarks made by employees concerning Headquarters City are viewed
with more credibility and consequently assigned more weight than any
print or film material sponsored by the Company. Therefore, it is
imperative that persons who meet with prospective employees be fully
prepared to sell Headquarters City in a <u>positive</u> manner, which means
going beyond making such neutral statemtments as "it's not such a
bad place to live."

Plant #1 City's location is more severe and probably more difficult to
resolve than Headquarters City's. The best solution may be to initially
conduct a study among our current employees and/or job candidates to
determine whether certain types of persons (such as those from smaller
cities and rural areas) are more likely to be satisfied with life in
Plant #1 City. If such types can be identified, then our recruitment
efforts could be redirected to focus on them. The second alternative
is to simply do a better job of selling the virtues of Plant #1 City.
Again, the responsibility for this task must primarily lie with those
persons meeting with the job candidates during their visit. If neither
of these two strategies are successful, and an otherwise favorably
inclined, highly regarded job candidate expresses strong reservations
about Plant #1 City, the only remaining strategy would be to emphasize
the Company's policy of horizontal movement--implying that the individual's assignment to Plant #1 City is not a permanent one.

-3- No matter which particular organizational characteristic is being "sold"
to the prospective employee, individuals having personal contact with
the interviewees during the on-site interview remain the principal
vehicles for selling the Company. Consequently, these salespersons
should be carefully chosen and briefed as to the importance of their
role and the factors which play an important part in most candidate's
decisions.

-4- The present study has shown that we can predict job candidates' responses
to our job offers with considerable accuracy (assuming the accuracy
generalizes to new samples). Consequently, corporate departments can
intervene with high quality candidates who seem likely to reject our
job offer, making a second effort to sell the Company by placing emphasis
on those areas the candidate has rated the Company as worse than other
firms. While it is very desirable to immediately place this tool into
actual use, it must be recognized that it is necessary to gather further
evidence of its utility on a new sample of job candidates. Therefore,
it is recommended that both strategies be carried out during the 1977-
78 recruiting season. That is, the candidates should again be questioned
about objective and subjective organizational characteristics immediately
following their on-site interview, with those responding split into two
groups. The information from the first group should be made available

. . . Continued

THE COMPANY

to departmental personnel for possible intervention use, and the information from the second group should be held aside to determine what level
of accuracy is attained in predicting their response to our job offers.
If a high level is again attained, then it would be recommended that
the questionnaire's use as an intervention tool be made a universal
practice in subsequent years.

-5- Finally, it must be concluded that this year's study has provided
valuable insights into the reasons underlying job candidates'
decisions to reject or accept our job offers. Thus, its diagnostic
value alone (independent of its intervention value) supports its continued use. Therefore, it is recommended that a questionnaire study
of the attitudes and beliefs of our job candidates regarding the Company
be made a permanent fixture of our recruitment process.

(Note: An abbreviated version of last year's questionnaire has been prepared
and is available for distribution if either of the latter two recommendations are accepted.)

TABLE 1

JOB CANDIDATES' VIEWS OF THE C.* AS A
WORKPLACE FOLLOWING THEIR JOB OFFER DECISIONS

Organizational Characteristic	Mean Value (4-point scale)	% Rating THE C.* Better Than Other Firms	% Rating THE C.* Worse Than Other Firms	% Rating THE C.* No Different Than Other Firms
Work Climate	3.2	55	7	38
Advancement Opportunity	3.1	38	21	41
Salary	2.9	36	19	45
Career Development	3.1	36	21	43
Varied Interesting Work	3.1	31	10	59
Growth/Stability of Company	2.8	29	2	69
Responsibility & Challenge	3.2	26	7	67
Location	2.3	24	24	52
Benefits	2.6	24	10	66
Skills-Job Match	3.1	17	10	73

Note: The sample size for this analysis was 42

*THE COMPANY

TABLE 2

Ratings of THE C.* Work Locations by Job Candidates Following their On-site Visit

Location	% Rating THE C. Better than Other Firms	% Rating THE C. Worse than Other Firms	% Rating THE C. No Different than Other Firms
Headquarters	26	36	38
Research Laboratory	33	38	29
Plant # 1	27	55	18
Plant # 2	60	10	30
Plant # 3	25	15	60

*THE COMPANY

212

TABLE 3

Job Candidates' Views of THE C.* as a Workplace Following their
On-site Visits, Broken Down by Department and Work Experience

| Organizational Characteristic | Corporate Department | | | | | | | | Work Experience | | | |
| | Corp. Engr. | | R & D | | Manufactur. #1 | | Manufactur. #2 | | Experienced | | Inexperienced | |
	%THE C. Better	%THE C. Worse	%THE C. Better	%THE C. Worse	%THE C. Better	%THE C. Worse	%THE C. Better	%THE C. Worse	%THE C. Better	%THE C. Worse	%THE C. Better	%THE C. Worse
Work climate	50	14	72	8	51	6	50	3	65	10	49	7
Advancement opportunity	44	11	48	20	40	11	62	9	51	12	53	14
Salary	28	8	40	8	17	6	22	12	32	7	25	10
Career development	17	6	24	4	11	9	25	3	20	0	21	8
Varied and interesting work	39	8	44	16	43	17	25	9	39	7	37	14
Growth/stability of company	28	11	36	8	26	6	38	16	46	17	44	9
Responsibility & challenge	22	11	24	0	29	6	50	9	25	4	29	5
Location	47	36	32	36	31	20	19	31	17	22	33	38
Benefits	39	11	36	20	11	9	28	9	49	12	26	12
Skills-job match	19	6	12	8	23	9	38	9	32	7	23	7

Note: The data reported in this table are based on the following sample sizes: Corporate Engineering = 36;
R & D = 25; Manuf. #1 = 35; Manuf. #2 = 32; experienced candidates = 41; inexperienced candidates = 146.

*THE COMPANY

TABLE 4

Importance Ratings Assigned Information Sources by
Job Candidates Following Their Job Offer Decisions

Information Source	Average Importance Rating*
Peers, family members	2.6
College professors	2.1
THE C.'s* campus recruiter	2.5
On-site interviewer(s)	4.6
Company publications	2.7
General print/broadcast media	2.4

*Scale values: 1 = no importance
                2 = slight importance
                3 = moderate importance
                4 = high importance
                5 = extreme importance

*THE COMPANY

214

IX. PERSONNEL MANAGEMENT & EMPLOYEE RELATIONS REPORTS

32.   [Co-op Students]

(Anonymous)

THE COMPANY: This report was provided by a major U.S. manufacturing company with headquarters in a large midwestern city.

THE REPORT: One valuable source of well-qualified new personnel is a carefully managed co-op program. This report is one company's evaluation of its co-op program and contains suggestions about how that program might be improved to make it more valuable for both the company and the co-op students. (The names of the company and the locations have been changed at the request of the contributing company.)

THE COMPANY

September 22, 1977

Manager College Recruitment

The following comments are offered in response to your memo of August
22, 1977, and our subsequent discussions.

Our co-op program currently involves 14 positions (12 engineering, 1
industrial technology, 1 auditing) at the following locations.

      ENGINEERING   -- Corporate Engineering 2 (may consider 3 during fall,
                                                winter and spring)

                       R&D - 3

                       Plant #1 - 1

                       Plant #2 - 2

                       Plant #3 - 3

                       Plant #4 - 1

      INDUSTRIAL TECHNOLOGY   -- Plant #1 - 1

      AUDITING   -- Headquarters - 1

Co-op rational patterns vary from school to school. We have accommodated
students on both semester and quarter academic calendars.

A listing of co-op work assignments describing specific projects or work
assignments or responsibilities by location has not been compiled. It is
recommended that such a historical list be made for the four quarters
beginning Fall, 1976 to Summer, 1977 and that this list be updated at the
conclusion of each quarter. More complete data are needed to monitor the
quality of assignments and effectively administer the co-op program.

It is recommended that managers now responsible for extending offers to new
college graduates develop a list of competencies desirable for new employees
and that co-op assignments be designed to provide opportunities for developing
such competencies. Development of skills may then be appraised more objectively,
facilitating decisions on both hiring co-ops after graduation and continuing
them from work period to work period. Coordinating the sequence of assignments and controlling the total number of assignments are critical to the
planning of such a program.

As it now exists, the program for chemical engineers requires students to
rotate to three different work settings. Students complete one work assignment
at Corporate Engineering, one work assignment at the R & D, and one work
assignment at a field location. Prior to March, 1977, students began the
program at any of the above three work situations. From discussions with

supervisors and co-ops who had progressed to advanced stages of the program, it was determined that an initial assignment at a plant provided a better foundation and orientation for an understanding of engineering applications than initial assignments at Corporate Engineering or the R & D Lab.

A standard pattern for subsequent assignments has not been established. Rotations have been individualized to accommodate preferences and requests by engineering personnel and students. Engineering personnel at Plant #3 have stressed the value of continuity and requested that students return to Plant #3 for as many assignments as possible. Student requests have frequently been based upon positive or negative experiences at a particular work location.

The number of work assignments available varies directly with eligibility requirements established by co-op schools. The number of assignments varies from four at the one university (students begin co-op assignments after completion of the sophomore year) to seven at two other universities (students may begin co-op assignments after completion of the freshman year). The advantages of seven available work periods may be offset by the minimal number of technical courses completed at the end of the freshman year. In the past, students have worked as few as two assignments because they began to co-op during their junior year or changed co-op employers.

If it is accepted that engineering students will in general work a minimum of four work periods and that the first work period is a plant assignment, then the following basic patterns for rotation are possible:

    Plant - R & D - Corporate Engineering* - Plants (same location)
                                                    (second location)

    Plant - Plant (same location) - R & D - Corporate Engineering

    Plant - R & D - Plant (same location) - Corporate Engineering
                          (second location)

    *Generally agreed to best be scheduled after lab assignment

It is recommended that these sequences be discussed with engineering managers. The different patterns might best be linked with specific locations or the co-op rotation pattern at specific schools.

In addition to an analysis of the relative merits of the above rotational sequences, it is recommended that an analysis be made of the rotational plans scheduled by co-op schools. The number of work periods required, credit hours required for participation, and the pattern of work periods are important consideration for this analysis.

217

Manager College Recruitment   -3-   September 22, 1977

Problems in scheduling students may arise if co-op school patterns are
incompatible. Six-month work periods may be difficult to integrate with
three month, or quarter-length assignments. A three-month project which
is begun by one student and easily continued by a second student who also
works a three-month rotation may not be as suitable for one co-op who works
six months at a time. It is recommended that extended assignments provide
opportunity for development rather than one three-month assignment twice.

It is recommended that schools be identified for future co-op recruitment
activities on the basis of rotational pattern and the number of work
assignments included in the co-op program.

It is recommended that a study be made of the co-op programs at the
universities selected for the recruitment of engineering graduates. Future
co-op recruitment might best be planned to supplement our efforts at schools
selected for intensified activity. It is recommended that the role of the
campus co-op coordinator also be determined. A coordinator who advises students
on prospective employers, provides guidance on scheduling courses, and often
counsels students on matters relating to work assignments may provide
assistance in the selection of new co-ops and planning for subsequent assignments. Co-op programs may be administered by individual academic departments
or administered from a central department. A program administered by the
engineering department may likely be coordinated by a faculty member and
provide more informed referrals of high quality co-op candidates.

It is recommmended that if new co-op schools are selected for recruitment
efforts, new co-ops be hired from these schools only as attrition requires.
Increasing the number of co-op positions at locations at this time is likely
to complicate efforts to coordinate assignments as discussed above.

No criteria have been established for the selection of new co-ops. Minimum
GPA guidelines have not been set. Selection has been based primarily on
career goals and motivation as determined in a personal interview. Recommendations
from co-op coordinators have also aided College Recruitment personnel in the
selection of new co-ops.

Our chemical engineering co-op program has been administered on the corporate
level. College Recruitment has had responsibility for hiring new co-op
students and coordinating the rotation of assignments.

During the 1976-1977 academic year nine chemical engineering co-ops were
recruited from five universities. One student who had participated in the
Summer Minority Pre-Freshman Program and one student who participated in the
Minority Visitation program were also hired as co-ops. A listing of all
co-op students is attached.

As the number of participants in the Company's other student programs, specifically the Summer, Pre-Freshman Minority, and Minority Visitation programs has increased, the number of students progressing from one program to another has also increased. It is recommended that criteria for eligibility be coordinated if such progression is to be a planned goal.

It is recommended that a policy be formulated to clarify the purpose and intent of the Company's varied work opportunities for students. For summer programs it should be determined if our goal is to:

  a) encourage students to return for a second or third summer

  b) provide a one summer experience

  c) screen candidates for co-op employment

If students are to be encouraged to return for additional summer assignments, then it is recommended that repeat assignments at one location or a progression of assignments at different locations be examined.

If students are to be selected for one summer, and if the summer program is also a recruitment activity to identify high quality students before formalized college recruitment begins, then it is recommended that we employ only those students who have completed their junior year of school. It is also recommended that an effort be made to recruit these summer students from those colleges selected for intensified college recruitment activities.

If the summer program is intended to be a screening period for co-op selection, then it is recommended that:

  a) the work experience be of a quality that will encourage interest
     in co-op employment

  b) formal criteria be established for acceptable performance

The co-op program for students who are not majoring in chemical engineering can be divided into three distinct categories: other engineering disciplines, industrial technology, and accounting.

At the present time two mechanical engineering majors and one material science major are participating in the co-op program. One mechanical engineering student participated in the Minority Pre-Freshman Program prior to beginning the co-op program. The other mechanical engineer participated in the Minority Visitation program. The material science major, recruited directly from a University as a chemical engineering student, changed her major after her first work assignment at Plant #3. Engineering personnel at the Plant approved her return.

It has not yet been determined if the rotational pattern presently required of chemical engineering co-ops is also appropriate for other engineering students.

To date, the material science major has worked two co-op periods at Plant #3, with assignments in the Environmental and Project Engineering groups. Both mechanical engineering majors worked their first assignments at Plant #3; one as a co-op and one as a pre-freshman. The first has since worked at Plant #1 and is currently assigned to Corporate Engineering. The second mechanical engineering student worked in the Reliability group at Plant #3 and returned for a co-op assignment at Plant #3 for the fall quarter and has requested to again work in the Reliability group.

It should be noted that we have not actively recruited co-op students who are majoring in mechanical, electrical, civil, or other engineering disciplines for our co-op program. It may be unwise to permit only minority and female students from such engineering disciplines to co-op with us.

At the present time, two industrial technology co-ops (1 female, 1 male) were hired by the Plant #1 after graduation. Students majoring in industrial technology co-op only at Plant #1. One co-op is employed per work period in the Reliability/Inspection group.

All students have attended an area university. Typically one or two students have been referred per work period. Plant personnel interview and hire. They have recently requested that we initiate contact with departments of industrial technology at other universities to increase the number of candidate referrals.

The Auditing department now provides one co-op position per work period for students majoring in accounting. The department prefers students who have completed their sophomore year of school. College Recruitment initiates referrals from two local universities. Auditing department personnel interview and hire.

The Marketing group has also initiated plans for the development of a co-op program. Co-op positions in both industrial and agricultural marketing are under consideration.

The current programs for the Reliability group at Plant #1 and Auditing department as well as the proposed program for Plant #4 are intended to recruit and develop employees for specific departmental positions. The engineering co-op program with its rotational structure provides a pool of candidates for consideration by engineering managers at four plant locations, Corporate Engineering, and Research and Development.

The administration and coordination of such a pool program presents special problems. Competition between participating departments for high potential co-op students is likely. It is recommended that procedures be developed to coordinate requests by students for specific assignments with requests by managers for students to return to their department. Such requests are likely each time co-op students alternate from school to work assignment. Coordinating the interests of co-op students and department managers for offers of permanent employment after graduation is an extension of this activity. The interface of co-op programming and College Recruitment is critical at this point.

It is recommended that College Recruitment be responsible for the overall
coordination of the Company's co-op programs in order to best complement other
recruitment activities. Within the structure of such a system, requests by
departments for developing a co-op program would be submitted to College
Recruitment. College Recruitment would provide guidance on the design of the
proposed program and work assignments. Recruitment of co-op students and
hiring procedures are best specialized to the needs of participating
departments.

IX. PERSONNEL MANAGEMENT & EMPLOYEE RELATIONS REPORTS

33. Equal Opportunity, Your Company and You

(Tyson Foods, Inc.)

THE COMPANY: Located in Springdale, Arkansas, Tyson
Foods, Inc., processes and markets poultry
and other food products. The company employs approximately 7,000 people.

THE REPORT: A well-defined and fairly-implemented advancement program is one very effective
method of assuring high employee morale
and productivity. The following report
is Tyson Foods' memo to its employees ex-
plaining its advancement program.

222

Tyson Foods, Inc. DRAWER E • SPRINGDALE, ARKANSAS 72764 • TELEPHONE (501) 756-4000

June 26, 1972

TO: ALL EMPLOYEES

SUBJECT: Equal Opportunity, Your Company and You

Equal Opportunity is the law. Basically, this means that discrimination toward any person as to employment, upgrading, demotion, rates of pay, training, etc., based on religion, color, race, national origin, sex or age is prohibited. In addition, as a supplier of products to the U.S. Government, we are required to take affirmative action in job categories where we are deficient in the use of minority group persons and women.

As a result, we have established a staff position to review our employment policies, our current situation, and establish affirmative action plans at all locations with goals and time tables to correct deficiencies. Part of this action requires that the Company advise all employees of its affirmative action policy in order to create equal opportunity awareness. While this is the law, I am pleased to point out that your Company has not needed to be prompted by the Government in the recognition of our obligations. "The Principles of Our Employment Relations" has long stated our policies in these areas as we provide that: "Equal consideration will be given to all employees regardless of race, sex, color, religion, national origin or age. It is what the individual <u>can</u> and <u>will</u> do to contribute to the progress of our business that matters."

Nevertheless, a simple policy statement does not necessarily assure understanding or change old concepts and habits. So, let me put it this way, regardless of your race, sex, color, national origin, religion or age, you will be considered for any job in our Company for which you are qualified when opportunities occur. In addition, where training is provided, you will not be denied it for any of these discriminatory reasons.

As you know, promotion does not occur simply as a result of length of service. In fact, as we also state in our "Principles," seniority "combined with our needs to use the maximum of <u>ability</u> on all jobs is necessary to maintain high product quality at competitive cost." Furthermore, while your records indicate your experience and skills, employees do have the obligation to advise us of their job interest in order that we might qualify them. That is the purpose of our "Application for Promotion," (sample reproduced below) so that we can be advised of your job interest when we have vacancies or new positions.

This form can be obtained from your supervisor. When interested in promotable opportunities, it should be completed in full and submitted to your supervisor during which time you may discuss your experience and qualifications. If unqualified, your supervisor will permit you the opportunity to learn the job in question during temporary vacancies. Hereafter, when a job at a higher than base classification is permanently vacated, that job and its qualifications will be posted on the bulletin board. Employees interested in filling that position should write their name on the posted bulletin or otherwise notify their supervisor of their interest. The job will then be filled whenever possible with the most qualified senior employee who has filed an Application for Promotion form for that position. The successful bidder will be the employee who properly performs the job according to management's established standards. The employee must meet the requirements of the job as the job will not be changed to meet the limitations of the employee.

I hope you will avail yourself of opportunities as they occur in our Company as it is only experienced, qualified employees who will make us successful. Additional information and answers to questions may be secured from your supervisor.

DON TYSON
Chief Executive Officer

APPLICATION FOR PROMOTION

NAME_____   DATE_____

Present Job_____   Department_____

Department Seniority_____

I would like to apply for promotion, as a result of a permanent job vacancy, for the position of:_____

In Department_____

My qualifications are (list other jobs that you have performed satisfactorily, skills, or experience with other employers):
_____
_____
_____
_____
_____
_____

Supervisor's Acknowledgment of Qualifications:_____

1. Employees in the department where the vacancy occurs, and who have filed an Application for Promotion, will receive first consideration.

2. All applications will be reviewed on the basis of seniority-ability as provided in our posted Seniority policy.

3. Employees transferring from one department to another will go to the bottom of the seniority list in the new department, while keeping their hiring date for purposes of layoff protection, vacation, and other benefits.

REVISED 5-25-72

THE PRINCIPLES OF OUR EMPLOYMENT RELATIONS

The Management of Tyson Foods, Incorporated, has the responsibility to provide a fair return on investment to Stockholders <u>and</u> Employees through a profitable business.

For the Stockholders, the return on the investment of their savings for our use is a fair return of interest.

For the Employees, the return on the investment of their time, skills, and energies is fair treatment in wages, benefits,...and, in their daily association with us.

To realize the maximum growth, with security, our policies in regard to all parties must be, and will be, consistent with these responsibilities.

To effectively work together toward our goal of PROGRESS WITH SECURITY, all of our Employees, Supervisors, and Management should understand not only our basic policies, but the principles or reasons that support them:

1. Wages and Benefits: We will maintain a program that is competitive: that is, influenced by (a) industry patterns at each location; (b) changes in the general economy; and (c) conditions of our business. To do anything less could result in losing the interest and service of experienced, dependable Employees. To do anything more could result in pricing ourselves out of our competitive industry and thereby jeopardize our business and our jobs.

2. Seniority and Ability: The seniority of Employees will be recognized in proper balance with ability. Employee's loyalty and interest, combined with our needs to use the maximum of ability on all jobs, is necessary to maintain high product quality at competitive cost...and that is what creates customer demand, and our growth.

3. Promotions and Job Opportunities: Equal consideration will be given to all Employees regardless of race, sex, color, religion or age. It is what the individual can do and will do to contribute to the progress of our business that matters.

4. Grievance and Problems: Every Employee has the right to a prompt, open-minded reception and thorough reply to his grievance, suggestions, or questions. Only through a complete understanding and discussion of mutual problems can Employees and Management develop confidence in each other and work in harmony.

5. Orderliness and Discipline: In the interest of efficiency, safety, and for the protection of the individual, reasonable rules of conduct are applicable equally to all Employees. The proper enforcement of rules must be taken to protect the majority of Employees from the abuses of any indifferent few.

6. Communications and Information: The most important personnel duty of Management in regard to Employee relations is the communication of information. Primarily, this will include information concerning Employee rights, benefits, and obligations. However, for the fullest realization of our goals, it must also include information pertaining to our business, our problems, and our mutual responsibilities.

Our commitment to these principles with the interest and cooperation of our Employees, should provide the maximum of PROGRESS WITH SECURITY...where everyone works toward the PROFIT objectives that provide our jobs.

TYSON FOODS, Inc.

34.   Career Planning/Development Worksheet

(Quaker Oats Company)

THE COMPANY: Although it is best known for its food pro-
                 ducts, Quaker Oats Company also produces
                 pet foods, toys, specialty chemicals, and
                 art needlecraft supplies. The company is
                 also in the restaurant business. Company
                 headquarters are in Chicago, Illinois.
                 Quaker Oats employs approximately 30,000
                 people.

THE REPORT: This memo introduces a revised career plan-
                 ning/development worksheet and suggests a
                 schedule for implementing an evaluation
                 procedure based on information gathered
                 with the new forms. Following the memo
                 are samples of the letters introducing
                 the program to lower level supervisors and
                 employees and a sample of the worksheet
                 itself.

QUAKER

October 29, 1979

TO: Mr. Daryll Kalek:

CAREER PLANNING/DEVELOPMENT WORKSHEET

As agreed, I have revised the subject form to satisfy our needs for establishing training and development plans.

The form satisfies these important needs:

1. The employee is permitted to "voice" his or her objectives and needs.

2. The wording of the form (see question #1) is designed to discourage unrealistic goals on the part of low potential employees.

3. The form minimizes administrative work on the part of supervisors in that the only paperwork they would have to complete is question #4 in the joint session with the subordinate and a brief summary of the discussion with the sub-ordinate.

This form could be used for all exempt employees regardless of their promotability. Since we would have to assume that the majority of your people are promotable, it was designed with them in mind. Non-promotables would be handled differently only in the sense that the one-on-one session with the supervisor would include appropriately candid feedback.

The process, if you agree, would work like this (the dates being tentative):

November 7:   Daryll Kalek meets with all departmental supervisors to explain program and ratio-nale.

November 14:   Memo goes out from Daryll Kalek to depart-mental employees introducing activity, rationale (see sample Attachment A).

November 19:   Employees receive the worksheet with cover letter signed by direct supervisor (see sample Attachment B).

November 23:   Employees return questionnaire to
                    supervisor with items 1-3 completed
                    (question #4 to be completed in one-
                    on-one session).

November 28:   Begin one-on-one sessions between
                    supervisors and subordinates. (Super-
                    visors write up informal summaries
                    of the discussion immediately after-
                    wards and retain for own use in future
                    discussions and planning).

December 1, 1979   Carry out training and development
      thru   plans.
December 1, 1980:

January 1, 1981:   Repeat cycle.

I think this approach could work very well in your department,
Daryll, and I'm ready to discuss anytime.

Chris Main

Christine C. Main
Personnel Manager
Corporate Office

CCM:de
Attachments

QUAKER

Sample Letter from Department Head introducing Program.

TO: All departmental Employees:

Nearly all career-oriented people periodically stop to ask
themselves what the future holds in terms of their professional
development. As a result some people may lay out specific
career objectives and plans while others may, for a variety of
reasons, continue to pursue ambiguous goals. Regardless of
how we answer this question, most of us are interested in
achieving our highest potential.

Quaker has an interest in your career planning, too. We want
our people to develop their careers in a way that maximizes each
person's talents, ambitions, and satisfaction.

Toward this mutual end, we are introducing a systematized approach to career planning that will encourage open discussion of
this important subject between employees and their supervisors.

Next week you will receive a questionnaire that asks you to
respond to a few questions regarding your career objectives and
developmental needs. The questionnaire will be accompanied with
additional information on how the process will work.

I see this Program as one that will benefit all of us through
a sharing of information, and will give us the opportunity to
step back from our day-to-day activities and give some thought
to your next few years at Quaker.

                        Daryll Kalek
                        Director - Corporate Services

QUAKER

Sample Letter from direct supervisor to subordinate

TO: (employee's name)

As Daryll Kalek announced in his memo last week, the department
is implementing a simple systematic approach to career planning
that gives employees and their supervisors an opportunity to
focus discussion on this important subject.

Attached is a Career Planning/Development Worksheet. The purpose of this worksheet is to get your input regarding your career
objectives and developmental needs. Please complete questions
1-3, and return a copy to me by November 23.

(secretary's name), from our department will then set up a
meeting for the two of us to discuss the worksheet. Please come
prepared to complete question #4 together. Suggestions for this
item might include activities you can do on your own (i.e. course-
work, reading, etc.) as well as those the Company can provide in
the way of seminars, assignments, or other developmental activities.
It would be a good idea to bring along your copy of the worksheet.

Let me know if you have any questions regarding completion of the
worksheet.

                        Signed by supervisor

CAREER PLANNING/DEVELOPMENT WORKSHEET

EMPLOYEE'S NAME _____

PRESENT POSITION _____ MONTH/YEAR _____

1. BASED UPON YOUR PERFORMANCE AND EXPERIENCE IN YOUR CURRENT
   JOB, WHAT WOULD YOU CITE AS YOUR CAREER OBJECTIVE OVER THE
   NEXT 1-2 YEARS? *

2. IN WHAT SKILL/KNOWLEDGE AREAS DO YOU FEEL YOU NEED IMPROVEMENT?

   A. IN ORDER TO PERFORM MORE EFFECTIVELY IN YOUR PRESENT
      POSITION?

   B. IN ORDER TO BE CONSIDERED FOR A PROMOTION?

*Responses to this item may include 1) new assignments, projects,
or experiences within scope of present job, or 2) another position
in the department/Company which represents a lateral or upward move.

3. WHAT SPECIFIC WORK ASSIGNMENTS, TRAINING ACTIVITIES, OR SUPERVISORY ASSISTANCE DO YOU FEEL WOULD HELP MEET YOUR OBJECTIVES?

4. THIS SECTION TO BE COMPLETED JOINTLY BY YOU AND YOUR SUPERVISOR.

DEVELOPMENT PLANS FOR NEXT TWO YEARS

	ACTIVITY	DATE
1.		
2.		
3.		

35.   Dining Room Hostess Evaluation
         [with Job Description]

(Chart House [Burger King])

THE COMPANY: Chart House, Inc. is in the restaurant and
                fast food business. The Burger King Cor-
                poration is one of its restaurant chains.
                Corporate headquarters are in Lafayette,
                Louisiana. Chart House employs approxi-
                mately 13,000 people.

THE REPORT: In addition to evaluating individuals,busi-
                nesses must periodically review particular
                jobs to determine if they should continue
                to be filled. In this report the managers
                at Chart House ("CHI") are evaluating the
                position of Dining Room Hostess in Burger
                King restaurants. Appended to the report
                is the job description for the position.

MEMORANDUM
July 25, 1977

TO: Michael F. Valenta

FROM: Floyd W. Collins

RE: DINING ROOM HOSTESS EVALUATION

As per your request, I have reviewed the concept of utilizing
Dining Room Hostesses in our Burger King restaurants. Listed
below are my opinions, calculations and field surveys regarding
your question, "Are we getting our money's worth from the Dining
Room Hostess program?"

The recently implemented standard labor formula provides for
36 direct labor hours of Dining Room Hostess service per restaurant each week. On a company-wide basis, the cost of this
program is approximately $1.2 million annually. [1] Should the
minimum wage be raised to $2.65 an hour, the program would cost
CHI $1.36 million annually. [2]

In reviewing the Dining Room Hostess job description, the hostesses'
primary responsibility should be one of interaction with customers.
The summary job description is as follows:

> The Dining Room Host/Hostess is a prime "image personifier"
> of Burger King restaurants and is responsible for welcoming,
> seating and fulfilling the customers' additional food service
> needs, as well as distributing premiums to our customers.
> The Dining Room Host/Hostess must convey enthusiasm,
> friendliness, and courtesy to the customer to insure con-
> tinued patronage.

Of the approximately eight or nine specific duties and responsibilities,
six involve customer greeting and assisting on the part of the
hostess. A copy of the job description appears at the end of this
report.

Michael F. Valenta
Page Two
July 25, 1977

A survey of operations in the field seems to indicate that
Dining Room Hostesses are not performing their primary responsibility as defined in the job description. In reality,
the Dining Room Hostess spends the majority, if not all, of
her time cleaning tables in the dining room. When not cleaning
tables, the hostess was observed returning to work in the kitchen.
A copy of the field survey is attached to this report.

The possible reasons for the divergence in Dining Room Hostess
activities, from what is intended as described by the position's
job description and what work is performed in actuality, vary.
Perhaps store managers are not aware of the responsibilities of
such hostesses. Perhaps store managers do not realize or are
skeptical of, the value of hostess interaction with customers.
Again, perhaps Dining Room Hostesses are supplementing kitchen
labor because of a shortage of help in that area. Whatever the
reason, from the limited store samples taken, it appears that the
Dining Room Hostesses are not providing CHI Burger King restaurants
with the primary service intended by that position.

Michael F. Valenta
Page 2A
July 25, 1977

1.   269 restaurants
        x36 hours of dining room hostesses per week
      9,684 hours per week

      9,684
      x 52 weeks per year
    503,568 hours per year

      503,568
      x 2.40 estimated average hourly wage
    $1,208,563 cost of Dining Room Hostess program to CHI

2. 503,568 hours
         2.70 hourly wage + uniform allowance
     $1,359,634

RESTAURANT DINING ROOM HOSTESS SURVEY

STORE - SAMPLE OBSERVATIONS:

Friday, July 15th - Store 1537 - 11:35 to 11:55
The hostess (I presume) came out of the kitchen area
and spent all of her time cleaning tables. Not once
did she greet or thank a customer, assist a family
or children, or ask any customer about the quality of
the food. The hostess was well groomed although she
wore the same red and yellow uniform as the counter
hostesses and kitchen employees.

Monday, July 18th - Store 1537
Observed hostess for approximately ten minutes. Her
primary job was the cleaning of tables, although
she assembled one high chair top. When I asked to see
the store manager, she was cordial and friendly in
her response and immediately ushered me back to the
manager's office. The hostess was well groomed.

Monday, July 18th - Store 241
Spent approximately 30-35 minutes in the unit observing.
The hostess entered the dining room from the kitchen,
cleaned tables for ten minutes and returned to the kitchen.[1]
The hostess was not well groomed. She looked as if
she had been laboring over a hot stove.

1. No other work or services were performed in the
   dining room area.

Monday, July 18th - Store 1548
Observed for approximately fifteen minutes. Hostess
came from the kitchen area, cleaned all the dirty tables,
and returned to the kitchen. The hostess did obtain a
cup of ice for a customer seated in the dining room
when asked by the customer. She did not provide Burger
King crowns to any of the children in the dining room.
The hostess was well groomed.

Michael F. Valenta
Page Four
July 25, 1977

Thursday, July 21st - <u>Store 241</u> - 11:00 to 1:15
   The hostess was cleaning tables when I arrived. After
   the tables were cleaned and the napkin dispensers
   were refilled, the hostess returned to the kitchen.
   While the hostess was in the dining room, a customer,
   with her child in her arms, had to pull a high chair
   across the dining room without any hostess' assistance.
   In addition, no crowns were offered to the several
   groups of children in the dining room. The hostess
   did not greet nor assist any customers.

JOB DESCRIPTIONS

DINING ROOM HOST/HOSTESS

I. SUMMARY DESCRIPTION

The Dining Room Host/Hostess is a prime "image personifier" of Burger King Restaurants and is responsible for welcoming, seating, and fulfilling the customers' additional food service needs, as well as distributing premiums to our customers. The Dining Room Host/Hostess must convey enthusiasm, friendliness, and courtesy to the customer to insure continued patronage.

II. BASIC OBJECTIVES

A. The incumbent should be customer-oriented, possess an excellent appearance and have an outgoing personality.

B. The individual should be even-tempered and respond to stress situations in a mature manner.

C. Above all, the incumbent should be children-oriented, as a great deal of this position's responsibilities center upon rewarding and catering to children and their families.

III. JOB RELATED KNOWLEDGE

The individual should have a knowledge of all menu items and prices. Experience in restaurant customer service and child care and handling are also important attributes for this position.

IV. SPECIFIC DUTIES AND RESPONSIBILITIES

A. When possible, the Dining Room Host/Hostess should meet the customers at the entrance of the Dining Room and welcome them personally to the restaurant.

B. When feasible, the Dining Room Host/Hostess should direct or assist the customer to a table that is spotless and has been supplied with a clean ashtray and a full napkin dispenser. If there are toddlers, a clean and sanitized high chair or booster seat should be placed next to the table. The high chair tray should be covered with plastic wrap, under which should be the premium(s). The Dining Room Host/Hostess may assist the parent in seating the child, and place a crown on the child's head.

240

DINING ROOM HOST/HOSTESS

    C. The Dining Room Host/Hostess is responsible for maintaining all premiums (i.e., rings, puppets, crowns, balloons, etc.); extra packets of condiments and coffee, all on a serving cart for distribution to the customer at all times.

    D. The Dining Room Host/Hostess will be responsible for serving an extra cup of coffee to those who have ordered coffee.

    E. Continuity of customer contact is important; therefore, when possible, cleaning minor spills is the responsibility of the Dining Room Host/Hostess. As major areas need cleaning (i.e., dining room floor, trash containers, windows, and rest rooms), the Dining Room Host/Hostess should bring this to the attention of the Restaurant Manager.

    F. Direct customer complaints to the Restaurant Manager.

       NOTE: Notify the Restaurant Manager, immediately of <u>any</u> emergencies, i.e., customer illness or accidents, disputes between customers, etc.

V. <u>KEY POINTS OF THE POSITION</u>

    A. The employee must be well groomed and neat in appearance.

       <u>NOTE:</u> Refer to SPI 7107.06, Employee Appearance and Behavior in this manual.

    B. The employee should, when possible, welcome the customer.

    C. The individual is responsible for handing out the children's premiums, and offering adult customers extra service, i.e., condiments and an extra cup of coffee.

    D. Maintain all premiums, condiments and coffee on the special serving cart in a neat and orderly manner. Be sure you have sufficient supplies at all times.

    E. Make certain high chairs or booster seats are sanitized, and that premiums are ready for distribution to the children. Assist in seating children.

    F. Restock the serving cart with all premiums, condiments and coffee after peak sales periods.

    G. Never argue with a customer. Always direct the Restaurant Manager to the customer concerning any complaint.

    H. Sincerely thank and invite the customer to return.

IX. PERSONNEL MANAGEMENT & EMPLOYEE RELATIONS REPORTS

36.   Supervisory Back-up Plan

(Anchor Hocking Corporation)

THE COMPANY: Anchor Hocking Corporation manufactures
                 glass products, plastic and ceramic drink-
                 ware, dinnerware, decorative hardware,
                 glass and plastic industrial components,
                 and packaging. The company employs approx-
                 imately 17,000 people. Its headquarters
                 are in Lancaster, Ohio.

THE REPORT: Not having trained, experienced people
                 ready immediately to take over key super-
                 visory positions when they are vacated can
                 severely disrupt a company's operations.
                 This report introduces to the managers of
                 Anchor Hocking a plan to ensure the com-
                 pany will always have people qualified to
                 step into those key positions and thus
                 avoid the confused, inefficient operations
                 that had characterized the interval between
                 the departure of a manager and the full
                 orientation of a successor.

G. C. Barber   R. L. Hollaway, Jr.

    SUPERVISORY BACK-UP PLAN   September 25, 1975

cc: M. W. Hatfield - Plant 10
     D. F. Brown   - G.O.

Attached is a copy of the subject that was developed by a committee of three
Plant Managers and D. F. Brown. This plan was approved at the last Plant
Managers' Meeting and the plants are budgeting accordingly for 1976. You will
note that it involves eleven back-up people being trained for eight major
positions. The three large plants will be responsible for training two people
each, and the small plants will be responsible for training one person each.

If you have any comments or disagreements with this plan, please advise.

mns   R. L. Hollaway, Jr.

Attachment

SUPERVISORY BACK-UP PLAN

INTRODUCTION

Our Division does not have a consistent supply of qualified, experienced and available supervisory personnel to fill vacancies as needs arise. The following are examples of the situation:

. Production Superintendent - Winchester (Position vacant (6) weeks - no internal candidates).

. Supervisor - Mix & Melt - San Leandro (replaced by transfer from hourly, no pre-supervisory experience).

. Manager-Mechanical Services - Houston (replaced by hire from outside).

Recognizing this problem, a committee of three Plant Managers was organized to develop a positive program to provide for future superivsory needs in certain Key Positions.

PLAN OBJECTIVE

The objective is to have properly trained personnel for designated positions who will have received sufficient training and be willing to transfer geographically to fill vacancies without loss of effectiveness in performance at the assigned unit.

THE PLAN

The following is a list of the eight major positions most in need of back-up personnel:

                    *Supervisor-Forming
                    *Supervisor-Mix & Melt
                    *Supervisor-Select & Pack
                     Supervisor-Mould
                     Supervisor-Carton
                     Plant Engineer
                     Supervisor-Maintenance
                     Industrial Engineer

*Two back-up candidates would be placed in training for these positions.

Each plant has been assigned the responsibility for training selected
back-up candidates for the above positions.

The following is a schedule of the back-up training assignments:

Winchester	Plant Engineer Supervisor-Carton Assembly Operators
San Leandro	Supervisor-Forming
Connellsville	Industrial Engineer Supervisor-Mix & Melt
Salem	Supervisor-Mix & Melt Supervisor-Select & Pack
Jacksonville	Supervisor-Select & Pack
Los Angeles	Supervisor-Mould
Waukegan	Supervisor-Forming
Houston	Supervisor-Maintenance

A. Candidate Selection

Back-up candidate selection would be a joint process involving Plant
Container Division Management inputs. Internal candidates throughout the company would be given first choice before recruiting from
external sources.

B. Orientation & Training

1. An orientation program will be given to each new back-up supervisor whether recruited from a school, transferred from hourly
or transferred from another plant.

The orientation program would consist of an introduction to all
facets of plant operation by spending limited time in each department. Following this the candidate would be assigned to the specific department for which he/she has been chosen as back-up.

245

The candidate would spend approximately four to five months in the assigned department to gain more in depth knowledge of the department operations. During this period the candidate would travel to Lancaster to meet with personnel in the assigned technical area at Division Offices, as well as meet with appropriate members at the General Development Laboratories. After six months, the back-up candidate would be given a specific assignment in the department, e.g., Foreman, so definite responsibilities can be assigned to enforce the learning process and make the individual a productive member of the unit.

C. Training

Each plant will be responsible for the development of a training outline for the back-up position(s) assigned.

This would be accomplished through the development of a thorough Position Analysis. Afterward a Comparative Analysis and Development by Objectives schedule is completed to insure that training is directed at specific areas needed by the back-up candidates. (This process is outlined in the Container Division Manpower Planning Program). As candidates progress their training could be expanded by having them travel to different plants on matters such as tank heat-ups, equipment installation, and special projects.

The overall orientation and training process would total 18-24 months to have candidates prepared as qualified back-up personnel.

FOLLOW-UP

Monitoring and appraisal of performance will be the responsibility of the individual plants. Quarterly Progress Reports will be prepared by the

candidates for review by appropriate plant personnel, Plant Manager
and Division Management for the first year and semi-annually the following year.

REPLACEMENTS

When a candidate is assigned a permanent position in another location,
the Plant will fill the training position with another person for continued training of back-up candidates.

BUDGETARY REQUIREMENTS

Each plant will be responsible to budget for the designated position(s)
and all salary, travel, and fringe benefit expense would be charged to
the training unit.

mms   D. F. Brown
September 17, 1975

X. REPORTS ON BUSINESS ETHICS

During the 1970's, because of the numerous public scandals involving corporations and their officers, American business executives became increasingly sensitive to the need for maintaining high ethical standards and making those standards public
knowledge. Even those companies with clear records
have taken positive steps to ensure that their corporate images are not tarnished by either unscrupu-
lous employees out for self-gain or well-meaning employees who perpetrate unethical acts in ill-advised
attempts to "help" the company.

Beyond this internal check on ethics many companies have made public statements outlining their
concept of corporate ethics. Often they have felt
the need to clarify even the nature of their business
operations to avoid any misunderstandings that might
lead some to criticize them on ethical grounds.

The reports in this section illustrate both internal guidelines on corporate ethics directed to employees and statements for the general public about
particular operations that some might question.

X. REPORTS ON BUSINESS ETHICS

37.   [Memo on Commitment to Ethical
         Business Practices]

(Media General, Inc.)

THE COMPANY: Located in Richmond, Virginia, Media Gen-
                  eral, Inc. employs approximately 4,400
                  people in various communication services
                  including newspapers, radio and television
                  broadcasting stations, cablevision opera-
                  tions, and printing services. The company
                  also offers financial services.

THE REPORT: This report is Media General's explanation
                  of the ethical standards it expects its
                  employees to follow. The memo is obviously
                  designed to protect the company's position,
                  but notice that in many places it also
                  functions to protect employees' interests
                  by pointing out potential problems they
                  might not otherwise see. The importance
                  Media General attaches to the issue of cor-
                  porate ethics is evident in the request for
                  a returned signature to verify that each
                  employee has read this document.

Alan S. Donnahoe
President

20 January 1977

Memo to: All Officers of Media General and its Subsidiaries

Gentlemen:

Media General consistently has sought to maintain the highest ethical standards possible in all of its dealings with suppliers, customers, and governmental agencies.

Many news items have appeared recently concerning revelations by major corporations of bribes and improper payments to government officials and others, both in the United States and abroad.

While I previously have announced that Media General will not tolerate or condone such practices (September, 1976 M/G News), the Board of Directors, at its November meeting, requested that I write a letter to our key executives re-emphasizing this Company's commitment to ethical business practices.

Please note carefully the following eight points:

1. Media General, and all of its subsidiaries, will comply with all applicable laws wherever it does business. We shall seek to comply not only with technical requirements but also with the spirit of the law.

2. Neither Media General nor any of its subsidiaries will maintain or establish any undisclosed or unrecorded fund (or asset) for any purpose.

3. No false, misleading, or artificial entries in the records or books of Media General or any of its subsidiaries shall be made or tolerated for any reason.

4. No payments to any supplier or person rendering service to Media General, or any subsidiary, shall be made in a manner intended to conceal the receipt of the payment by such person.

5. The payment or delivery of anything of value, or the furnishing of services or facilities, by or on behalf of Media General or any of its subsidiaries to a person associated with a Media General supplier or purchaser is prohibited, if the purpose of such payment is to induce the person to take any action by or on behalf of the supplier or purchaser, for the benefit of Media General or a subsidiary, or to influence such action, or to reward the person for having taken or influenced such action. This does not prohibit the giving of nominal gratuities, entertainment, or favors as courtesies in the normal course of business, so long as there is no suggestion that any act or favor is expected in return. If you are in doubt in any given case, refrain from taking the action.

6. No employee of Media General, or any subsidiary, shall accept anything of value of any nature from a present or potential supplier or customer of Media General, or any subsidiary, if the employee suspects that a purpose of the donor is to induce the employee to take or influence any act by Media General or any subsidiary for the benefit of the donor or the organization which he represents, or to reward the employee for having done so. This does not prohibit receipt of nominal benefits given openly in accordance with ethical business practices, or receipt of benefits based on personal friendships, but does prohibit receipt of any benefit which may appear to influence business acts by Media General, its subsidiaries, or their employees. If you are in doubt in any given case, do not accept the gift.

7. The payment or delivery of anything of value, or the furnishing of services or facilities by or on behalf of Media General or any of its subsidiaries to any official or employee of a domestic or foreign government or regulatory agency is prohibited, if a purpose of such payment is to induce the official or employee to take or influence any official act, or to reward him for having taken or influenced such an act. While business courtesy should always be maintained, employees of Media General and its subsidiaries should seek to avoid any hint of impropriety, real or imagined, in their dealing with government officials and employees.

8. The direct or indirect use of any Media General funds or other assets, or the funds or assets of any subsidiary, for political contributions of any kind, or the establishment or administration of any committee or other organization for the raising or making of political contributions, within or without the United States, is prohibited, except to the extent any such activity is expressly authorized by resolution of the Board of Directors of Media General, or the Board of Directors of the appropriate Media General subsidiary.

It is the responsibility of each officer of Media General and its subsidiaries to assure that all personnel under his or her supervision are reminded of our policy of ethical business conduct which this letter reaffirms.

Anyone having knowledge or information of any prohibited undisclosed fund or improper payment should promptly report the same to me, or the Company's Controller, J. Curtis Barden. No employee need fear reprisal or loss of job for reporting any improprieties by a superior or another employee.

Media General has never been involved in the type of improper payments or political contributions which this letter outlines; and as our operations grow, it is your duty to ensure that Media General, and all of its subsidiaries, continue to maintain this same high standard of business conduct.

To insure that this letter has been received and read, will you please sign one copy and return it to me.

Sincerely,

Alan S. Donnahoe
President

ASD/k

Received and read by:

Title:_____

Subsidiary:_____

_____   Date: _____

X. REPORTS ON BUSINESS ETHICS

38. IBM Operations in South Africa

(IBM Corporation)

THE COMPANY: The IBM Corporation manufactures and markets business machines, electronic data
processing systems, electric typewriters,
copiers, and dictating equipment. IBM's
headquarters are in Armonk, New York. The
corporation employs approximately 310,155
people.

THE REPORT: Because of the racially repressive policies
of the South African government, certain
groups and individuals have placed considerable pressure on corporations to termi-
nate operations in that country. IBM's
response to this pressure is the following
report which defends its continued presence in South Africa on ethical grounds.
IBM's argument here is that its presence in
South Africa is more beneficial to the
black population than its absence would be.

IBM OPERATIONS IN SOUTH AFRICA

IBM Corporation
Old Orchard Road
Armonk, New York

February, 1980

IBM has been in business in South Africa since 1952. As of December 31, 1979, we had 1,442 employees there, mostly engaged in the sales and service of data processing equipment and office products -- work calling for high skill levels. IBM has no manufacturing operations in South Africa except for a small card printing plant with fewer than ten employees. Revenues from our South African affiliate are less than one percent of IBM's total annual gross revenues.

IBM Employment Practices

IBM gives equal pay for equal work. Its employees work in a non-segregated environment. Paid vacations, holidays, auto-purchase loans, pensions, group life insurance, tuition refund, dental, medical and hospital coverage are provided for all employees.

Through home loans guaranteed by IBM, black employees can buy, build and improve their homes. As of December 31, 1979, 38 employees had built new houses or had them under construction. An additional 31 employees had taken loans to purchase or improve their existing homes. Black employees also receive free technical advice on building and improving their homes.

IBM continues to increase its nonwhite employment in South Africa. In 1969, there were 39 blacks, or 4.6% of our work force. Total nonwhite employment was 6.7%. As of December 31, 1979, there were 187 blacks, or 13.0%, and a total of 255 nonwhites, or 17.6%.

Because high-level skills are required for many of the jobs in marketing and servicing information processing equipment, IBM recruits university graduates mainly. But in 1978, for example, only 801 blacks, out of a population of 20 million, earned college and post-graduate degrees. IBM is helping with the specialized training necessary for blacks to move into professional and technical careers. In 1979, 640 student days of classroom training were completed by black IBM employees to develop skills for careers in programming, customer engineering, general business administration and finance. Today, black IBM employees are working as data processing and office products customer engineers; switchboard operators; system programmers; computer operators; systems engineers and sales trainees. Four blacks are managers.

IBM Contributions to Black, Asian and Colored Education

Most of IBM's contributions in South Africa since 1972 have been to black institutions. In the past two years, of $546,000 in IBM contributions, $390,000 have gone to black beneficiaries. The largest grants are for black education and training. Some recipients:

-- The Chamdor Training Center near Johannesburg, which offers training in typing, secretarial skills, welding, salesmanship, motor repair and maintenance, and customer engineering basic training. An IBM employee has directed the center for more than four years, and IBM has donated equipment and a residential unit.

-- The Inanda Seminary near Durban, where IBM has donated two
   30-person classrooms and facilities for training black
   secretaries, and continues to give scholarships.

-- The University of Zululand, where a senior IBM manager was
   on loan to develop a data processing and systems analyst
   course leading to a diploma.

-- The Molapo Technical Training Center for high school students
   in Soweto, where IBM has donated a lab for teaching basic
   electrical and electronic skills. An IBM customer engineer
   works part-time as an adviser to guide the teaching of
   electronics at Molapo, and also at Chamdor.

-- Garankuwa Technical Training Center near Brits, where
   IBM has provided typewriters for training black secretaries.

-- Operation Upgrade, the organization that trains black
   instructors in a special technique for teaching black adults
   how to read and write. IBM has donated equipment and funds.

-- Dloko Higher Primary School, a black school near Durban.
   IBM has helped fund instructors, books and buildings, and
   supports evening adult education sessions. This effort was
   the forerunner of a program under which other companies have
   so far adopted ten black schools.

-- A scholarship program, under which university and high school
   students receive IBM scholarships. These include teacher
   training scholarships.

In addition, by the end of 1980, IBM will have provided $3 million
over three years in support of two other black education projects.

In Project Pace, IBM has joined with the American Chamber
of Commerce in South Africa, and other American businesses,
to fund a five-year commercial high school for 600 students
in Soweto. Construction is scheduled to begin this year and
the school's first enrollments are planned for January, 1981.
The school will also be used in the evening for adult education
and as a community center. IBM has pledged $300,000 toward
the capital cost of the school.

IBM has contributed $2.7 million toward a program to upgrade the
qualifications of black high school teachers in three subjects,
mathematics, physical science and biology. With better qualified
teachers, the standard of education will be improved. The initial
phase will include the purchase of videotape players to be installed
in teacher training colleges. IBM will supply relevant educational
films and videotapes acquired from international sources. Where this
material is not available, IBM will arrange to have videotape programs
produced in South Africa with the assistance of the best teachers
available. Once the project has been proved successful, IBM plans to
extend it into the high schools. The project has received enthusiastic
acceptance from teachers and the Ministry of Education and Training
and should have wide impact in South Africa.

Six Principles

In March of 1977, twelve major United States corporations--IBM
among them--with affiliates in South Africa announced their
support of a statement of principles (often referred to as the
Sullivan principles) aimed at ending segregation and promoting
fair employment practices at their plants and other facilities
in that country. As of December, 1979, 135 companies had announced
their acceptance of these principles as a way of doing business in
South Africa. These principles are consistent with IBM's employment
practices in that country.

The statement of principles follows:

STATEMENT OF PRINCIPLES OF U.S. FIRMS WITH
AFFILIATES IN THE REPUBLIC OF SOUTH AFRICA

1. Non-segregation of the races in all
   eating, comfort and work facilities.

2. Equal and fair employment practices
   for all employees.

3. Equal pay for all employees doing equal
   or comparable work for the same period
   of time.

4. Initiation of and development of training
   programs that will prepare, in substantial
   numbers, blacks and other nonwhites for
   supervisory, administrative, clerical and
   technical jobs.

5. Increasing the number of blacks and other
   nonwhites in management and supervisory
   positions.

6. Improving the quality of employees' lives
   outside the work environment in such areas
   as housing, transportation, schooling,
   recreation and health facilities.

We agree to further implement these principles.
Where implementation requires a modification of
existing South African working conditions, we
will seek such modification through appropriate
channels.

We believe that the implementation of the
foregoing principles is consistent with respect
for human dignity and will contribute greatly
to the general economic welfare of all the people
of the Republic of South Africa.

IBM Data Processing Installations in South Africa

Government accounts make up less than one-fifth of IBM's
revenues in South Africa. The great majority of IBM
computer applications, in both the public and private
sectors of South Africa, are those usually found in commerce
everywhere.

It is IBM's policy not to bid for business anywhere in the world
where it believes its equipment would be used for repressive
purposes and we know of no case where it is so used. However,
it would be misleading to suggest that any manufacturer can
control how its products are used. To our knowledge, no IBM
equipment or people are involved in the issuance and monitoring
of the passbooks that South Africa blacks are required by law to
possess. But any computer could be used for such a purpose without
the manufacturer's knowledge or consent.

Restrictions on Trade with South Africa

IBM abides by the 1963 and 1977 United States and United Nations
arms embargoes concerning South Africa. Sales of IBM equipment
to South Africa are in compliance with the United States
government's regulations. Among these are the following:

-- In December of 1976, the U.S. Department of Commerce revised
its export regulations to require individual approval for the
shipment of any data processing equipment to the South African
government's defense forces, police, or any agency responsible
for uranium enrichment. In June of 1977, the regulations were
extended to cover exports to the ministry which administers the
black passbook.

-- In February of 1978, the Department of Commerce imposed an
embargo on all U.S.-origin commodities, services and other
materials intended for ultimate use by South African military
or police entities in the Republic of South Africa or Namibia.

Critics have called upon IBM and other corporations to take a
variety of actions including: unilateral withdrawal from South
Africa; refusal to sell anything to the South African government;
refusal to sell to any South African organization any product
which could conceivably strengthen the economy.

For a corporation to undertake any of these actions for political
reasons is to inject itself into the conduct of foreign policy.
Any such action would set a precedent which no thoughtful American
should welcome: a precedent of taking foreign policy out of the
hands of government and putting it into the hands of corporations.

Citizens have the right to disagree with United States foreign
policy toward South Africa, and to work within our political
system to change it. But, in the absence of U.S. government
restrictions, corporations should be able to do business in
any country where they can treat their employees fairly and
operate in the best interests of the majority of their stockholders.

#   #   #

INDEX

(Roman numerals indicate section numbers; Arabic numerals indicate report numbers.)